Taking Care of *Your* Money

MULTI-DIMENSIONAL
INVESTING THAT WORKS

.

Taking Care
of *Your* Money

MULTI-DIMENSIONAL
INVESTING THAT WORKS

Brian K. Costello

ECW PRESS

CANADIAN CATALOGUING IN PUBLICATION DATA

Costello, Brian
  Taking care of your money:
    multi-dimensional investing that works

ISBN 1-55022-307-0

1. Finance, Personal. 2. Investments. 1. Title.
HG179.C67 1997   332.024 01   C97-931469-0

Design and imaging by ECW Type & Art, Oakville, Ontario.
Printed by Imprimerie Gagné, Louiseville, Quebec.

Distributed in Canada by General Distribution Services,
30 Lesmill Road, Don Mills, Ontario M3B 2T6.
Distributed in the United States by General Distribution Services,
85 River Rock Drive, Suite 202, Buffalo, New York 14207.

Published by ECW PRESS,
2120 Queen Street East, Suite 200,
Toronto, Ontario M4E 1E2.

http://www.ecw.ca/press

PRINTED AND BOUND IN CANADA

TABLE OF CONTENTS

Chapter 1

Multi-Dimensional Strategies That Work

Not everyone wants to be a millionaire.
Most people are content just to live like one.

Money talks

They say that money talks. Money doesn't really talk, of course. We all know that. But it certainly does matter. The trouble is that most of us aren't listening — or listening carefully enough — but those who do listen usually end up much better off than those who do not. It's simply a matter of education. It doesn't matter what the subject is — whether a sporting event or something you're teaching your child — those who listen simply do better. Usually much better.

My father taught me much of what I discuss in my books, at my seminars, and on radio and TV shows. What he was really talking about was multi-dimensional investing. His bottom line: invest in a way that you just can't lose. And the only way to make sure that you won't lose is to buy investments that pay off in more than one way.

It's really simple, and it's always been a great mystery to me why more people don't do this. Suppose you buy a stock that pays a high dividend. As long as that dividend keeps coming in — and you want to make sure that the company you're investing in has long-term stability — its stock will hold its value in the worst times.

I first heard about multi-dimensional investing as a youngster while picking cherries and peaches at my father's farm at Grimsby, near Hamilton, Ontario. My father had started his career with one of the big chartered banks but decided to leave after a few years for the uncertain life of a farmer. He thought it would offer more opportunity. It did. Working with the bank's customers over the years, he quickly reached two critical conclusions that changed his life forever — it's better to be an owner than a lender, and when it comes to investing, the best offence, as in sports, is a great defence.

My father had a constant stream of visitors in those days, including a couple of stockbrokers from Hamilton who would talk investment strategies with him while my brothers and I were busy picking fruit. Much of their talk centred on multi-dimensional investing — a term, by the way, that my father coined. This investment strategy made sense to me as a youngster, and even more today, and it has become the cornerstone on which I built my own investment philosophy. It has served me well. And it will you, too. It won't make you rich overnight, but if you start early enough, it can help you create a $1-million nest egg for your retirement.

How does it work? Basically, by choosing investments that offer more than one opportunity to profit. A blue-chip stock, for example, offers an opportunity to profit three ways — capital gains, a regular dividend income, and tax-advantaged growth and income potential. Unlike a stock such as Bre-X, for example, where you're risking everything on one throw of the dice, blue-chip stocks will eventually produce a capital gain. It's only a matter of time. And while it's marking time — or at a lower price than what you bought it for — you can bank on a regular dividend to sweeten the pot while you're waiting for the stock to go up again. And because the capital gain and dividend income is tax advantaged, you win no matter what happens.

It's a lot like buying a car with a sunroof. Before you take delivery, you should make sure the roof opens and closes. If it doesn't open at all, it's just a window in the roof. If it only opens, it's singular in dimension. If it opens *and* closes, you get the best of both worlds — sunlight and fresh air when the weather's great and daylight when it's cold or wet outside. But if you can't close it, your car will be virtually useless in winter or in a downpour.

Multi-dimensional investing is defensive investing at its best, and I tend to favour mutual funds for essentially the same reason — not all types of mutual funds, mind you, but those which offer capital gains potential as well as tax-advantaged income. Mutual funds offer two more advantages that I like — great diversification and a painless way to ensure that the dividends I earn are reinvested seamlessly and easily.

Multi-dimensional investing is a long-term strategy that focuses on you, your goals, and your investment style — above all, on the kind of investments that enable you to protect your capital in all markets. A multi-dimensional strategy will also help you avoid the two biggest traps most investors fall into at one point or another — chasing performance by buying the latest hot fund, and trying to time the market. Both strategies have a tremendous emotional appeal, but neither has produced out-standing results. We'll deal with this in greater detail a little later on.

My own investments have done very well because I've avoided one-dimensional investments that are supposed to go up tomorrow. Those kinds of investments are fine, I suppose, if investing is your only business and you're doing it day in and day out, but even then, sooner or later, you're going to get killed. That's what happened to the Campeaus and the Reichmanns and more recently to the investors, including some professionals, who loaded up on Bre-X. That's what comes from investing in something that is singular in dimension. When you fail to get what you were hoping for, you lose. And I don't like to lose.

I don't buy investments I think may lose. But because I don't always know the total picture about every investment I make, I choose a mixture so that even if I lose on one, another will pick up the slack. I may not — in fact, will not — make a killing, but I won't lose, either. And that, in my view, is a cardinal rule of investing. Once you invest a dollar, you can never get it back if you lose it.

How does this apply to a portfolio? Over the years, I've developed my own pecking order — mutual funds first, stocks second, and rental real estate third. All three are multi-dimensional. That includes tax advantages, which each offers in varying degrees. When developing my portfolio, I focus on investments that will also enable me to save taxes.

Most people are deluged with ideas from investment salespeople. It could be a high-flying stock like Bre-X, where you profit only if it goes up, or a gold stock like Barrick that will rise in price at some point but pays a dividend along the way. Or I could buy a mutual fund that would enable me to diversify my risk even more. It could even hold a stock like Bre-X, which some did, as well as a number of dividend-paying gold stocks plus dividend payers in other industries which would not be hurt if another Bre-X comes along.

With a classic multi-dimensional investment, you'll have a regular income coming in — income, by the way, that will enable you to buy more shares or units while you wait for your stock investment or mutual fund to go up in value. In the process, this strategy will reduce your overall cost through dollar-cost averaging — in effect, enable the fund to show performance even though it is not going up in value. When, however, it does go up, you'll be able to sell sooner — at a profit — because your original cost has been averaged lower.

I've taken this concept a step further and included tax planning. It wasn't as important to my father and his generation, essentially because they worked in an environment where tax rates were relatively low and interest rates quite high. All that changed over the past decade or so — to a point where if you can save 50% on your taxes, you effectively have a partner working with you: the government. That's the reason I make tax planning a critical element of my investment strategy. So should you.

If you have a good financial planner who can help you get your money out of your RRSP or RRIF without incurring a large tax liability, then you win going in and again when you're coming out. This way you can weather virtually any storm that comes your way.

Many people were conditioned by their parents to favour interest-bearing investments because they were "guaranteed." That's because their parents had gone through two consecutive decades of double-digit returns. That was then. This is now. And when you think about investing in fixed-income investments like GICs, think in multi-dimensional terms. If you're in a 50% tax bracket, for example, your investment must earn at least 7% before it starts producing a positive return once you subtract taxes and inflation.

It's quite clear, even from this simple illustration, that taxes must be included in any multi-dimensional strategy you adopt today. Think about investing as a business partnership that includes Revenue Canada in every activity you undertake. Instead of seeking out a 5% or 10% yield, you can get a 50% return by getting the government, as your partner, to give you back half the money you invest. This way, if you lose money, you'll be losing some of theirs, too, and, in effect, cutting your losses in half.

At the same time, however, you don't want to share half the profits with the tax collector. That's where a carefully crafted financial plan comes in — one that maximizes a multi-dimensional strategy.

This brings up another key point my father made over and over — if you want to make money, you must be an owner, not a lender. If you want to put your money in a bank, buy the bank's shares. Your return will be higher. Significantly higher. But I didn't know which bank was best. Then I learned that a mutual fund gave me the opportunity to buy shares in many of these institutions. Most equity-based mutual funds, in fact, always represent a significant holding of bank shares.

Here's another way of looking at it. If you buy a piece of gold, someday it may go up in value. If you buy gold stocks instead, the shares will produce dividends while you're waiting for the gold to go up. An even better multi-dimensional strategy is to put those shares or mutual funds inside your RRSP. Now you've got a tax deduction plus a regular flow of income while you're waiting for gold prices to go up.

That's what multi-dimensional investing is all about — investing with a strategy that keeps you in the driver's seat all the way.

Focus on your portfolio
— not on the "right" fund

Investment success has more to do with choosing the "right" portfolio than choosing the "right" fund. That sometimes gets lost in all the rhetoric about fund performance in up-markets, but two acknowledged experts in portfolio design — Gordon Garmaise and Allen B. Clarke — have plenty of statistical and anecdotal evidence to demonstrate otherwise in spades. Garmaise is president of Garmaise Investment Technologies and the architect of Mackenzie's popular Star Program, while Clarke is vice-chairman of AGF Trust and creator of two of the most successful "wrap" programs in the market — Richardson Greenshield's Sovereign Program and AGF's Harmony Program.

Garmaise's research shows that last year's hot performers actually have a tendency to underperform the following year. Out of 100 top funds in any given year, only 25 will survive as first quartile performers the following year; another 25 will slip to second quartile; 20 will drop to third quartile; while the remaining 30 will wind up in fourth quartile place.

So much for basing your fund selection on one-shot performance numbers.

"If we could choose the right fund with any regularity, the impact on our portfolios would be enormous — but that's not likely to be the case," observes Garmaise. "In fact, it's very difficult to beat the long-term return and risk of an asset class — essentially because there's so much randomness in the returns of funds within an asset class."

There is strong evidence, however, that there is a close relationship between how you weight your overall portfolio among various asset classes and how you do in terms of return and risk.

Both Garmaise and Clarke cite groundbreaking studies which show that long-term asset allocation accounts for some 90% of a portfolio's return. The balance — that's less than 10% — comes from the specific funds or securities you select for your portfolio and from short-term market timing (essentially tactical asset allocation), which has generally proved unsuccessful.

What has proved successful, they add, is strategic asset allocation — that is, selecting funds by asset type to deliver a return/risk combination you, as an investor, feel comfortable with.

The process starts, says Clarke, with a firm understanding of your risk tolerance — an understanding that goes well beyond a "gut" feeling or some vague notion of how you would behave if markets suddenly turned sour.

There are ways to determine your risk tolerance that are much more systematic than just guessing, including the use of specialty questionnaires and the like, says Garmaise. Star makes extensive use of a specially developed questionnaire in its program.

Once you've established your risk tolerance, the next step is to select a portfolio at the right risk level for you — one that has been "rigorously constructed" to get the best possible diversification out of the funds that are available today.

"The reason why that's important," explains Garmaise, "is that you can probably reach the same expected long-term returns by combining funds in a number of ways. The only difference is that the rigorously constructed portfolio will deliver those returns at less risk."

And risk is what it's all about. As a rule, higher returns equal higher risk.

But both Garmaise and Clarke are careful to point out that the market will only pay for a higher risk that is efficiently taken — risk that you cannot realistically diversify away any further.

"Once you start piling on additional risk after this point, all you're doing is assuming added risk without the promise of additional expected return," says Garmaise. This, in essence, is the thinking behind the development of both the Harmony and the Star Programs, where the most efficient portfolios are developed for investors in keeping with their individual risk profiles.

Investors can, of course, develop their own portfolios with the same concerns in mind. Ideally, they should do so with the help of a professional adviser who has access to both the tools and the methodology that will help them determine their risk tolerance — that's critical — and examine different portfolio possibilities.

A professional has a better shot at understanding which are likely to be optimal combinations to achieve an individual's investment goals in keeping with his or her risk profile than does that person working alone. Also, the adviser is there to help the investor follow up on the performance of each fund manager and to determine whether that manager is meeting the investor's return/risk goals.

How many funds are needed to achieve these results? No more than seven. This number will give you the best trade-off between risk and return. Varying mixes, depending on your risk tolerance, include Canadian equity funds, U.S. equity funds, Canadian and foreign fixed-income funds, international funds, emerging markets, and even derivative-based funds to provide additional foreign exposure — important in registered portfolios. Garmaise would add precious metals to certain portfolios. How much would depend on the individual. While precious metals are risky as investments, they do reduce the risk in portfolios because they're a good hedge against other asset classes.

Clarke and Garmaise also add geography to the equation. The importance of this type of diversification is not always clearly understood by investors. There's a perception among many investors that when the U.S. market is down, so are all other world markets. Not so, says Clarke. At certain times, some markets are overpriced and others are not, the point being that markets have certain levels of volatility and certain levels of rates of return.

Instead of focusing on this fund or that, investors would be further ahead, he thinks, concentrating on which equity markets they should be in and developing their portfolios accordingly. "This is not easy, either," says Clarke. "So what investors should do is buy into a selection of key markets around the world. This way you'll always be able to participate in a more broadly based market — with one essential difference: You are less likely to have down years and more likely to have moderate returns on an ongoing basis. Even your down years will be relatively minor."

This is strategic asset allocation at its best. Don't confuse it with tactical asset allocation, in which you decide what asset class or equity market will produce the best returns at any given time and structure your portfolio accordingly. This is much tougher to do, adds Clarke, and most investors are not good at it. Even among the most disciplined money managers, the returns are minimal at best.

"With an efficiently designed portfolio, you won't be the top performer. Or the worst. But you will get your fair share — without a lot of sleepless nights along the way."

What about doubling your money in five years?

It's possible, of course, very possible, to double your money in five years, and it's a great come-on and attention grabber — but it also may not be the way you want to do it. As a rule, the higher the return, the greater the risk. If you want to double your money in five years, you must also be prepared to accept a higher level of risk.

Basically, it boils down to your comfort level. That's crucial. If the fit isn't right, you'll end up selling at precisely the wrong time, usually after the market has sold off and you're in a loss position. The best way to find out when an investment will double is to use the **Rule of 72** — a simple yet effective tool that's been used by financial planners for years.

Here's how it works: Divide 72 by the rate of return and you'll find out how long it will take to double your money. If your investment earns 6% a year, for example, it will take 12 years for your money to double; if it earns 12%, you'll get there in six years.

What does it take to double your money in five years? Precisely 14.4% a year.

If you're not prepared to put your money into investments that produce these kinds of returns, then opt for a mutual fund, for example, that offers a level of risk and a rate of return you can live with — 10% a year, for example, will double your money in 7.2 years.

So the next time someone talks about doubling your money in five years, know what it entails — and make sure it meets all the requirements of your multi-dimensional strategy.

Always assess the risk first

The cutback in RRSP contribution limits has left many high-income investors scrambling for alternatives. And there are alternatives — some with more risk than others. So, before embarking down this road, get a clear idea of just how much risk you can handle emotionally. This will enable you to narrow the list down to a risk level you feel comfortable with.

A few investments can be made outside your RRSP and offer tax relief. These include labour-sponsored funds — but changes in the 1996 budget, including reduced federal tax credits and a longer holding period, have made them less attractive. There have been similar changes by participating provinces offering similar tax credits.

This would suggest that labour-sponsored venture-capital funds should be dropped from an investor's "approved" list — but that really isn't the case, either. Smart labour-sponsored funds are now switching their strategies and using their ability to attract funds and grow the investments they've made — providing you give them the time to work for you.

Let me digress briefly here to note that before looking at any tax-advantaged investment, you should use up all of your available RRSP contribution room first. **You should make that one of your golden rules.**

If you're choosing a labour-sponsored fund, the first thing you should look at is the quality of the investments it makes — in effect, how it will do without the tax relief. Treat it as a typical investment decision. If it's on a par with other investments, the tax relief is a bonus. Keep in mind, too, that it's a long-term investment. You have to leave your money in for eight years. Ask yourself whether the fund will be competitive with a typical mutual fund at the end of that eight-year period. If it looks as though it will be, think about buying it outside your RRSP. Here the tax relief is an extra that turns the fund into a great multi-dimensional investment which offers a good potential rate of return and excellent prospects for capital appreciation.

If it doesn't stand up as a good investment without the tax relief, then why even consider it? There are other investments out there, including a wide range of solid dividend-paying blue-chip equity funds, that do stand up without the tax relief. I know many investors rush into these funds without giving thought to these concerns. That's another reason I'm not a big fan of putting them inside my RRSP. My thinking is that if I do use them inside my RRSP, I would use the extra tax deduction to buy a good-quality mutual fund. This would give me some flexibility should I need to get out and have to forfeit the tax credits. Personally, I prefer to see labour-sponsored funds as investments outside my RRSP. This way I'm able to really compare investment to investment — with the chance for extra tax relief.

Oil and gas income funds, which offer Canadian investors special tax deductions, are also worth a look. These funds offer a 30% tax deduction in the first year. Thereafter, your investment should earn 10% to 12% a year, virtually tax-free because of continuing tax benefits.

Be careful, though. You don't want undue risk. You want a fund that buys oil and gas — not one that takes on the risk of drilling. Also, and this is important when dealing with oil and gas income funds, ask your financial adviser for a letter documenting past performance for previous purchasers, including original money invested, tax relief, income received, and today's value of the original investment. It's a great yardstick — and quite revealing.

In assessing these funds, keep in mind that oil and gas prices are not likely to drop significantly from current levels. In fact, there is a greater potential for them to rise at this point. This suggests to me that these funds are less risky than many other investments, providing, of course, they are not on the risky side — that is, where the main focus is on drilling. This is a bit too speculative for me. I know some people are prepared to take this risk on the chance of making a killing. That's why I recommend that you ask your financial adviser for a full report on the fund's track record.

In making your assessment — just as you would in the case of other tax-advantaged investments — ignore the tax relief for the time being and ask yourself whether you'll get your money back from the investment. For me, that's always the key. It's how well the investment does, not how well it does with the tax relief included. With 50% tax relief, you can make almost any investment look great. So dig deep.

I'm personally a big fan of oil and gas funds — just as I am of flow-through shares. These are common shares that qualify for special tax write-offs. This form of financing is used mainly to fund the exploration activities of mining, oil, and gas companies. When it comes time to sell these shares down the road, you pay tax on the full amount — as though you paid nothing for them. If they do well, you'll get a nice capital gain as opposed to taxable income. A great multi-dimensional investment from a different angle.

Real estate limited partnerships also produce substantial relief and hold considerable appeal for high-income investors. Whatever the investment, always keep in mind that saving taxes is only one part of the equation. No matter how big the tax deduction, it's not worth it if you don't get back your original investment, plus yield and tax relief.

Loss of capital is only one risk

There are two basic types of risk — loss of capital and loss of income generated by that capital. Most people, however, focus on the first — loss of capital — to the point where they sacrifice income without realizing that this kind of loss can be just as devastating on their retirement plans.

In 1995, for example, you might have earned 8% on a term deposit. Today, perhaps 5%. A $10,000 investment earning 5% will yield $500 in income. So does a $5,000 investment that earns 10%.

Many people have a hard time understanding this emotionally. They buy a term deposit or a GIC because they think their money is safe, without realizing that this type of investment comes at a price, and a big one at that. GICs are not guaranteed. Only the principal is — and then only up to $60,000. This point is important when you realize that the yield on GICs and term deposits has declined virtually every year since 1981. The loss in purchasing power would have been significant over this period, far outweighing any potential loss of capital.

Another point: As investors, we have no control over the loss in income associated with investments like GICs. In fact, the financial institution where we buy the GIC can invest our money anywhere it wants, even in the riskiest investments going, if that's the nature of its business. In effect, we investors are totally dependent on what it does with the money. The first $60,000, as noted earlier, is guaranteed, but remember, if the financial institution goes down, it may take some time before we see our money again.

If you're gun shy about making other kinds of investments, think about a high-quality blue-chip equity fund that has the potential to grow and give you an escalating rate of return, as opposed to the declining rate of return witnessed for almost two decades by investors who have put their faith in term deposits and GICs.

In the case of a good mutual fund, that declining rate of return has not been the case. If you're concerned about volatility, keep in mind that a loss is not a loss until you sell and realize the loss. It's really a simple matter of hanging on for a year or two, and you'll be well rewarded for letting all the positives of multi-dimensional investing do their work.

The Systematic Withdrawal Plan: Multi-dimensional investing at its best

There is a neat, simple way to maximize retirement income without incurring undue tax liability.

The Systematic Withdrawal Plan is unique to mutual funds, although, ironically, not well known or used. It enables investors to withdraw up to 10% every year from whatever mutual fund they have their money invested in without triggering any sales charges.

The balance of your money continues to gather capital gains and other investment income, often producing triple or quadruple returns over a 15-to-20-year period. The money could, in fact, produce income for as long as you live and provide capital for your estate. The trick is not taking out more than the fund earns in any one given year.

If, for example, you have $100,000 invested in a fund which earns 10% a year, you could withdraw $10,000 and leave your original capital intact. If the fund earned 20% — as many did in 1993 and 1996 — you could withdraw $12,000 without incurring any sales charges and add another $8,000 to your investment.

But that's only part of the equation. The following story will illustrate what I mean.

A relative of mine sold his home a few years ago for $200,000 and bought a condo for $100,000. I suggested he invest the

$100,000 that was left over in a mutual fund and take out a small amount every year under the fund's Systematic Withdrawal Plan.

At that time, he could have purchased a term deposit that would have paid him 12% or $12,000 a year. The Systematic Withdrawal Plan would have produced a similar income — but with a difference. The $12,000 income produced by the term deposit would have incurred a tax liability of $4,800 — compared with a tax of $175 on the same amount of income from a Systematic Withdrawal Plan.

There's no magic to it. Under the Systematic Withdrawal Plan, you're actually getting back your own money, plus a little interest income. With this plan, you receive back mostly principal in the early years so that your yield is allowed to grow for future use. Sooner or later, however, you will receive back all your principal, and at that time you'll be required to pay normal taxes.

This is an important consideration in terms of Old Age Security and other social benefits. Because you don't have to report this income on your tax return, you might very well escape the clawback provisions on Old Age Security as well as other social benefits that are most certainly in the works.

I know people who have taken all their money and invested it in a fund so they could then withdraw it under this plan. This has enabled them to qualify for the guaranteed-income supplement — even though they had a substantial amount of funds invested under this program. That situation changes, of course, after six or seven years — but in the initial years of retirement, at least, when we often need money the most, the tax liability is virtually zero.

Many investors, especially first-time mutual fund buyers, have a hard time understanding that they're actually earning a rate of return on their investment unless they actually see it in their bank accounts every year. That can create a tax problem. As soon as you earn investment income — whether in the form of cash or in extra units in the case of a mutual fund — it's taxable. If, however, you let the income grow inside the investment, as in a mutual fund, and withdraw the principal instead, the tax consequences are somewhat different.

Let me explain how it works: If you bought a 10-acre farm at $10,000 an acre, for example, your total cost would be $100,000. If you sell one acre for $11,000, that represents a 10% yield. What is your tax liability? It's not on $11,000 but on $1,000 because the first $10,000 represent a return of principal. This is important to understand because by getting back your principal first, you pay less tax.

That, by the way, is how your bank also operates. It lends you $100,000 for a mortgage on your home on which you make monthly payments made up of principal and interest. Do you think the bank pays tax on the principal and interest on each payment? Or just the interest? It turns around and lends that principal to someone else. The flow of money is tax-free. That's something we investors must learn to use as well.

As far as Revenue Canada goes, this applies only to non-sheltered investments. Much the same arrangements can be made to withdraw your funds from your RRSP — but it must be done through a RRIF.

Although many people start withdrawals as soon as they buy the funds, I think there's a lot of merit in letting the funds you've chosen get a year or two under their belts before you start making withdrawals. It's also best to diversify through several mutual funds. That way, you'll be using the ideas of two or three portfolio managers to protect your assets.

Now the acid test. Here are the actual results for three well-known funds. If you had invested $100,000 in Templeton Growth in January 1977 and withdrew a total of $364,283 over the next 20 years, your original investment would be worth $658,083.

In comparison, if you had invested in a five-year GIC during this period and had withdrawn $750 a month for 20 years, would your original investment still be worth $200,000? I think that by taking out $750 a month over this time period, you would have had to attack the principal at some point early on, given the level of interest rates over this period. In fact, whether there would be *any* principal left would be more to the point. Actually, your money would have run out in 1980. And after inflation is taken into account. . . . I'm sure you get the point.

Suppose you had invested that $100,000 in Mackenzie Industrial Growth in January 1968. After withdrawing 9% a year or $750 a month for 29 years — that's a total of $264,000 — your original $100,000 would be worth $2,017,956.

If your withdrawals had kept pace with inflation, which averaged 4% a year over the period, your monthly withdrawals in 1997 would have reached $2,039. This would have raised your total withdrawals to $486,052. Despite this, your original $100,000 investment would be worth $1,178,336.

If your $100,000 had been invested in Trimark Fund in September 1981, your original investment would have grown to $626,430 after 15 years. And that's after withdrawing 9.9% or $850 a month.

Similar examples can be shown for other funds.

Most people use the Systematic Withdrawal Plan for retirement purposes, but there are other uses, including university education as well as helping your children meet their mortgage commitments.

Strategies for the cautious investor — alternatives for GIC refugees

If you're nearing the age of retirement and you don't want to take chances, there are options, other than GICs, that can help you maximize returns on your retirement money.

The answer, quite simply, is a properly diversified portfolio. The makeup of the portfolio will depend on a number of factors, including risk tolerance, age, and how long your retirement funds must serve you and your spouse.

The key, as I have already noted, is diversification. The first step is to divide your money into five investments. That's all you really need. If you're ultraconservative, here's what I mean:

Keep 20% of your money in cash — money market mutual funds (T-Bills), and if you think T-Bills aren't safe, then put it in a savings account. You get next to nothing on your money, but it's instantly accessible. A good alternative is Canada Savings Bonds, but they only come out in the fall. Access to cash is important because one of the big problems people have is that when they want their money and can't get at it, they have to sell off something that's good — or worse yet, they have to sell off a good investment that's in a loss position.

Another 20% might go into a GIC or, preferably, into a mortgage-backed security. One of the problems with term deposits and GICs is that you're locked in. The only way out is to wait either until they mature — or until you die. I don't recommend the latter. A mortgage-backed security, on the other hand, can be sold at any time. In addition, there is no limit on the mortgage-backed security guarantee, and it pays a monthly income — so that you effectively have faster access to some of your money. In addition, when rates fall, mortgage-backed securities go up in value.

Take the third 20% and invest it in a Canadian mutual fund. Work with your financial adviser to find one that meets your risk tolerance and investment objectives, one with a good track record, one with a fairly high profile that's easy to track.

Invest the fourth 20% in a foreign mutual fund. Canada accounts for only 3% of the world's capital markets, so I'd make sure some of my money was in the other 97%. Historically, international mutual funds outperform Canadian mutual funds.

Also, international funds give you protection against potential fluctuations in the Canadian dollar.

So your only decision now is what to do with that last 20%, and your financial adviser will help you with that.

If you look at this portfolio, 40% of your money is in guarantees — money market funds, mortgage-backed securities, or GICs. Even your Canadian mutual fund will have a portion of its funds in T-Bills. If you feel you need additional guarantees, then take the last 20% and invest in money market funds or mortgage-backed securities.

Whatever the case, this mix will not only provide a superior rate of return than a simple GIC but will also give you greater flexibility in the process. It's multi-dimensional investing carried to the nth degree. Perhaps more than I would recommend, but it does illustrate the power of making your money work harder for you without undue risk.

Keep performance in perspective

Performance, as they say, is everything. Or is it? Performance is important — make no mistake about it — but not at the expense of your overall investment strategy or your long-term goals. I mention this because every year, it seems, there are one or two hot funds or markets that investors focus on, sometimes to the exclusion of their long-term investment objectives.

That is not to say that many of these investments aren't worthwhile, especially over the long term. Asian funds, hot performers in 1992 and 1993, turned out to be big duds in 1994 and for much of 1995, for example.

A lot of investors who bought these funds in 1993, on expectations of the same kind of returns in the future, weren't ready for the drop in fund values that dogged Asian markets for the next two years, with the result that many sold out — at a loss — in frustration.

Understandable. Very understandable. But if these funds had been bought as part of a long-term diversification and asset-mix strategy, they would still be holding on — and benefiting from the upsurge, which will probably be just as breathtaking when it comes. And it will.

Much the same could be said about emerging markets and Latin American markets, which fell out of favour with a devastating thud in 1994 but came roaring back to life in 1996. In 1995, technology and health-science stocks turned in super performances but retreated sharply the following year.

Bottom line: Whatever investment you make, be sure it fits your investment style, your time horizon, your risk tolerance, and, above all, that it's part of an overall strategy that focuses on portfolio performance.

Dollar-cost averaging can also play a role in these situations. If you're looking at the long term — and you have money in a few duds — think about selling some of these (if they're outside your RRSP) and taking a capital loss. This will enable you to wipe out capital gains on other investments you may hold. You can always buy these investments back — providing you wait 30 days — or another investment in a similar industry or fund. Now you can afford to wait for these investments to work their magic down the road, because markets do come back. Eventually.

Also, if you're reinvesting on a regular basis, you'll actually pick up bargains in these markets — so, in effect, you'll actually be lowering your average price. In fact, the combination of tax planning and dollar-cost averaging can really lower your average price, so you'll be able to make a profit that much sooner. With this strategy, markets only have to recover a small amount for you to be in a profit position.

That's one of the main reasons portfolio construction is so important. By focusing on your portfolio — and less on short-term performance — you'll be less concerned with this month's hot fund or the performance of a specific equity or bond fund and more with your portfolio's overall return. Over time, your returns will not only be higher, but you'll also sleep better at night.

Time, not timing

Every time stock markets go up, there's a feeling in the air that stocks will climb forever. And when they drop, pessimism takes over, and investors feel that markets will never recover.

Neither, of course, is true. In the past 150 years, there has never been a case where the stock market, if it went down, did not go back up. That includes the big crash of 1929 which heralded the Great Depression. Had you invested $10,000 in the market just before it went into a deep freeze, that investment today would be worth millions.

Closer to home, if you were caught up in the euphoria that pushed the stock market to new levels in 1987, and bought $10,000 worth of Trimark, for example, on the Thursday (October 15) before the markets went into a tailspin, you would have lost 40% of your money by the following Tuesday (October 20). That, by the way, was after the market had taken a 508-point hit the day before — the biggest one-day drop in market history.

Understandably, most people were panic-stricken. If you were able to get ahold of your financial planner, he or she probably would have reminded you that you were in for the long haul and that things would right themselves eventually. If you were holding stocks, you probably would have run for cover and taken your money and put it in term deposits to ensure that this never happened to you again. Unfortunately, most of the people who did precisely this only made matters worse, because GIC and term deposit rates have declined every year since then.

In dollar terms, you would have lost $4,000 on your original $10,000 investment — and much of the potential yield this money would have earned since then in the stock market. If you had hung on instead, your original $10,000 investment in Trimark would be worth about $32,000 today.

This is the worst-case scenario I know — a 40% loss immediately on making the investment at a time of great panic. If you had hung on, that investment would not only have recouped all that it had lost, but 10 years later it would have been worth three times what you paid for it. I can't think of a better reason to commit to a long-term investment strategy.

At the beginning of 1995, I was telling investors that markets were on their way to new highs. Shortly thereafter, you may recall, interest rates were raised and equity markets went into a tailspin.

What happened? A replay of 1987. Many investors, especially GIC holders, panicked and took $2 billion out of mutual funds and put their money into GICs and term deposits. A few months later, stock markets were back on track and went on to post new highs.

The result: The GIC investor earned 6% on his money, while the individual who hung on ended the year with high double-digit returns.

One final point. Templeton conducted a study on the performance of its growth fund from 1970 to 1995. It showed that if you had invested at the worst possible time every year — when the market reached its highest point — the average annual rate of return over the 25-year period was 17.1%.

Had you invested the same money in the same fund at the best possible time each year — that is, when the market reached its lowest ebb — the average annual rate of return for the period was 17.8% The difference — less than 1%.

In the real world, nobody hits the top or bottom. We're more likely to be somewhere in between, so that the real difference over

this period would be in the neighbourhood of three-tenths of 1%
— less than two-tenths after taxes. The lesson: Successful investing is a matter of time. Not timing.

$1 invested in 1800. Best bet?
Stocks by a wide, wide margin

While everybody is concentrating on the day-to-day markets,
we'd sleep a lot better if we looked over our shoulders and used
that information to predict what will happen to our money in
the future.

I'm constantly being asked by people what to do with their
mortgages, whether they should dump their mutual funds,
whether the dollar is going to collapse, whether, in fact, the
country is going to collapse.

It would be great to be a market timer and jump in and out of
the market from time to time. Most of us, however, wouldn't
survive. In fact, I suspect most of us would be buying at the top
and selling at the bottom. In the long run, you're better off buying
quality equity-based investments and hanging on to them for a
long time. They will pay off in the long run.

History shows that most investors are emotional about their
investments and, more often than not, tend to jump in — with
both feet — when markets are on a roll. The professional,
however, usually gets in when stock prices are low. This, again,
is one of the big advantages of using a professional — if only to
help keep your emotions out of the investment process.

Ideally, you should be buying when prices are low — at what
Sir John Templeton calls the point of maximum pessimism.
Investors, however, tend to shy away from the market at times
like this. If you had bought a vacuum cleaner for $200, for
example, and saw it on sale for $150 a week later, would you take

yours back and ask for the difference? And if you hadn't bought it the week before, would you be more inclined to buy it now? Price has a definite bearing on purchase decisions, although for some reason it seems to work in reverse when it comes to investments.

When it comes to investments, time heals a lot of wounds, especially in the financial world. A new set of numbers compiled by Jeremy J. Siegel, a professor of finance at the Wharton School of Finance at the University of Pennsylvania, was recently released in a book called *Stocks for the Long Run*, published by Irwin. The scope of the numbers and the results is absolutely amazing.

I regularly see charts cross my desk from brokers and mutual fund companies showing how their portfolios compare to stock indices. A good portfolio manager should outperform the markets. After all, that's why he or she gets paid.

Buying for the long term seems very compelling after speaking with Jeremy Siegel. In fact, combining long-term investing with a good portfolio manager is even better when you realize that diversification produces the best results over the long term.

Just imagine you had a relative living back in 1800 who had an extra dollar to invest. The first thing we have to consider is inflation. As we all know, it destroys the purchasing power of money. In fact, if we were to find that investment tucked away in Uncle Charlie's old trunk, we'd have to get at least $12.10 today just to break even. It doesn't sound like a lot when only one dollar is involved, but you can sure see the impact when you multiply it by thousands of dollars.

More importantly, it really says to us that our money has been destroyed 12 times since 1800. Ask yourself how many more times it will be destroyed in your lifetime if we are not successful in combating inflation.

One choice Charlie may have opted for might have been gold. We know gold has been a long-term store of wealth. One dollar's worth of gold purchased in 1800 would be worth about $1,570 today. And while gold fluctuates in price from time to time, it produces no yield. In addition, if you buy gold, you usually just put it in your safety deposit box and let it sit there while it goes up and down. You don't profit at all. You just ride it — nowhere — essentially because there is no reinvestment. Reinvestment should be one of the cornerstones of every investment strategy.

I think there are better choices. You couldn't do it today with $1 — but suppose Uncle Charlie bought $1 worth of treasury bills. Today they'd be worth $3,020 based on Professor Siegel's studies. So much for doomsayers who tell us gold is the place to hide your money in uncertain times.

Another safe haven would have been government bonds. From 1800 through to the mid-1920s, there wasn't much difference between treasury bills and government bonds, primarily because interest rates didn't vary much. From then on, however, the spreads have been much greater. As a result, the gains have been much more rewarding — so that $1 invested in government bonds in 1800 would be worth $7,830 today.

Part of that extra gain can be accounted for by reinvestment. While gold goes up and down from time to time, it produces no yield. As a result, there's nothing to reinvest. With T-Bills, the yearly yield and the principal were reinvested each year, so the amount would have gradually risen — even with the usual ups and downs in interest rates.

With government bonds, there are several advantages. Usually, the yield is higher than with T-Bills. However, if we sold those bonds today, we would also do a bit better in terms of tax.

Also, until 1995, only the first $100,000 in capital gains were tax-free. Today, 75% of our capital gains is taxable.

Talking about capital gains makes me think about stocks and mutual funds. Professor Siegel also studied the Standard & Poor's Index in the U.S. With 500 stocks, it's more representative than the Dow Jones Industrial Average, which is made up of 30 stocks.

The S&P Index is more like today's mutual fund and a better comparison than the Dow Jones Industrials because mutual funds didn't exist in 1800.

That $1 invested in the Standard & Poor's Index is worth $3,360,000 today. That includes sell-offs in 1840, 1907, 1929, and a few others over the past 197 years. But what a difference in the numbers — more than $3.3 million in profit through investing in stocks rather than bonds, T-Bills, or gold.

While none of us will last 197 years, we should all invest long-term. The markets will surge from time to time and decline once in a while, but over a reasonable period of time, they will always rise if you buy good-quality investments and diversify properly.

The real fundamentals of your portfolio

In all the talk about politics and economics, let's not forget the real fundamentals in your life — your home and your RRSP. These are the two cornerstones of your life — your principal residence, which rises in value tax-free, and your RRSP, which gives you tax deductions.

In the historical pecking order, owning a principal residence is more important than ever before — since Ottawa cancelled the $100,000 capital gains deduction. Sooner or later, most people will try to save some money for their retirement — in most cases, a little too late.

Owning a home could make a difference for many people who are within striking distance of retirement — especially those who were not able to put money aside during their 40s and 50s for their retirement years. The sale of their home, which has been rising in value all this while tax-free, means a bigger windfall — and the source of retirement capital in later years.

In today's interest rate environment, you should look at a third scenario — paying down your debt. This is a point a lot of people miss. If you have a loan on which you pay 10% interest, you should ask yourself what that 10% really costs you. If the loan is not a tax deduction, you may have to earn as much as 20% more to cover taxes and the loan cost.

Most people would be better off today if they cancelled out debts. In some cases, that may mean cashing in investments to pay off the debts. If they then borrowed to buy back the same investments or other investments, the interest on the loan would be tax deductible.

Here's the difference — instead of having to earn 20% more in pre-tax income to pay the interest on a 10% loan, the individual would be able to deduct the interest cost from her taxes. The real cost for this individual — 5% after taxes.

The biggest problem I find with people is that they want to hold on to some reserve money . . . in case the roof leaks. Result — they let thousands of dollars sit in low-paying savings accounts. What they should be really doing is paying down their debts and borrowing to acquire investments.

Always, always think long-term

When it comes to investing, it's hard to convince people to think long-term. They get caught up in the here and now, and base their decisions on when to buy or sell usually on emotion. And the result is usually the same, too — disappointment, whether the investment was guaranteed or not.

History, however, shows that if you take out the shortest-term investment you can — that's a savings account — you'll also earn the lowest rate. History also says that if you buy the longest-term investment you can, you'll find that time will work in your favour.

Think beyond the immediate. If you have a fight with your spouse, it doesn't mean you're headed for the divorce court. You get over it. You know the spat is temporary. The same thing applies to the stock market, mutual funds, real estate, or any other investment.

A prime example is your home. How many times have real estate prices gone down over the past 40 or 50 years? Yet people still make money by owning their homes. No one questions that. History has also shown that stocks and equity-based mutual funds always outperform the real estate market. Perhaps it's human nature, but most of us would rather take a negative, short-term view of most situations, particularly the stock market.

Some people solve this problem by putting some of their money in short-term investments for liquidity and investing the balance long-term to take advantage of capital gains prospects.

I maintain a portion in equity funds on a permanent basis because I know they will outperform other asset classes over the long term. I also keep a portion of my money in bond funds for the same reason. The funds are managed by investment professionals who are in regular contact, in the case of equities, with the companies they're interested in. They take this information and compare it with other companies in the same industry. Armed with this information, they are often able to move in or out of an investment long before the rest of us get wind of the changes. That's what you should be focusing on.

For better returns, get used to the ups and downs

When it comes to the stock market, ups and downs are a fact of life — so learn to live with them if you hope to make the most of your savings.

Over a 10- or 15-year period, stock market investments beat anything else out there hands down — and that includes bonds,

GICs, or real estate — so you really can't afford to be out of them.

Still, market declines, particularly a steep drop like the one we had in 1987, can be unnerving and make it very, very difficult to keep your perspective. You have to keep remembering that stock markets don't go down forever; eventually, they bounce back, often with considerable vigour.

An interesting study on market declines, published by Mackenzie Financial, showed that, above all, declines are more common and less devastating than you would think. In fact, notes the study, the market has dropped by 5% at least twice a year — 127 times — over the past 50 years. Market declines in the order of 10% or more occurred once every 18 months or 33 times over this period. Significant corrections — of at least 15% — occurred once every three years or 16 times during this period. Last occurrence — August 1990. Major declines, during which the market dropped by at least 30%, occurred once every five years or nine times over the period. Last occurrence — October 1990. These, of course, are only statistics and should not be used to try to outguess the market. No one has ever been able to do that with any degree of success.

To me, the study is important for what it doesn't say — that no matter how many times the market has declined and no matter by how much, it always comes back, stronger than ever.

And if there is a lesson, it's this — if you're in the market for 10 or 15 or 20 years, it doesn't matter what it does today, this month, or even this year. What does matter is what it will do for your savings in the next five or 10 years. That's where your focus should be.

Where will today's superstars be tomorrow?

Every year there's one fund or group of funds that produces spectacular results. If you had the foresight to have bought a resource fund when base metals were about to take off, for example, you know precisely what I mean.

The same applies to funds that specialize in energy stocks or a small-cap or an emerging-markets fund. Some of these have produced returns of 100% or more in a year.

Yesterday's darlings, however, may not be tomorrow's super-heroes. If you bought one of these funds when it was in full flight, you know how devastating a precipitous fall from grace can be.

The real question is whether these funds, with their spectacular rises and, quite often, bone-chilling drops, offer a better return over a 10-year period, for example, than funds that turn in respectable but unspectacular returns year after year.

The answer isn't quite clear-cut. I've picked seven funds at random to illustrate what I mean:

AGF Canadian Resource Fund, for example, rose 96.2% or at an average compound rate of 7.2% a year over the 10-year period covered in the study.

Trimark Fund, on the other hand, rose by 164.3% over the same period or at a compound rate of 15.4% a year.

Templeton Growth Fund, another consistent performer over the period, posted a 159.9% gain — equal to a compound annual rate of 14.9%.

Mackenzie Industrial Income Fund, whose prime focus is on income rather than on growth, rose 113.7% or by 12.9% a year.

AGF Japan Fund increased by 143.7% or by 12.2% a year, while Dynamic Fund recorded an average compound rate of return of 12% a year or a total of 132.2% over the period.

A notable exception was C.I.'s Pacific Fund, which produced spectacular returns on three occasions during the same period, rising a total of 249.7% or 21.6% a year during the 10-year period covered in this study.

In dollar terms, the results are easier to see: $10,000 invested in AGF Canadian Resource Fund would have been worth $20,100 at the end of the 10-year period; Trimark Fund would have risen to $44,863 during the period; Templeton Growth Fund, to $40,066; Mackenzie Industrial Growth, to $33,725; AGF Japan, to $31,745; and Dynamic Fund, to $31,050.

Personally, I look for funds that produce good — but not spectacular — returns year after year. Track performance is crucial — if not by the fund, then certainly by the fund's portfolio manager.

What's a fair time period by which to judge track performance? One year certainly isn't enough. Three years? Five years? Ten years? As a rule, the longer we can track a fund's or a portfolio manager's performance, the better.

With the proliferation of new funds — in the past two or three years in particular — this will not always be possible. In those cases, take a hard look at the track record of the fund managers. While this is certainly not a guarantee that their performance will be duplicated in an entirely new environment, it is an indicator — and only an indicator.

Chapter 2

RRSP Razzle Dazzle

Two things to remember about money:
The mint makes it first.
It's up to us to make it last.

Keeping your goals on track

RRSP season is a good time to review your portfolio with your financial adviser and find out if you're on track.

Is it living up to expectations? Is it generating the kind of returns needed to meet your retirement objectives? Is it diversified to minimize downside swings and to make the most of strong markets? Are you comfortable with the volatility? And the asset mix?

In answering these questions, especially those about performance, keep in mind that mutual funds are long-term investments and that **no manager should be judged on a single year's or even two years' performance.**

As a rule, I shy away from running after the latest flavour of the month. My preferred strategy is to find a manager with a good track record — in all markets — and stay with him or her until there's a compelling reason to sell.

How, then, should you construct your RRSP portfolio so that it reflects your approach to investing, your risk tolerance, and, above all, your retirement goals?

First, decide on what funds you should keep or buy and the criteria you consider critical to the process. I personally place a lot of emphasis on a fund manager's investment philosophy — whether the fund manager is value- or growth-oriented, and whether I'm comfortable with his or her approach to stock selection.

As a rule, I choose funds with complementary investment management styles. This is because the market rewards both styles — but at different times — and often shifts its emphasis from one to another, usually without warning and, quite often, all in the same year.

If all your money is in growth and the market is rewarding value, don't expect your fund to produce the same level of returns as we saw in 1996, for example, when dividend funds — the bluest of the blue — turned in spectacular performances. That's great if you happen to hit it dead-on but not so great if you're out of sync.

The solution: Put part of your money in value and part in growth. This way, you're not betting all your chips on one style or another.

But if your resources are limited, and you have to choose one style or another, opt for value.

This is borne out in a U.S. study, which bases its conclusions on more than 40 years of stock data to compare value vs. growth investing. The study showed that the best way to outperform the market over time was to stick with stocks with low price-to-book (the underlying value of the shares) value ratios and low price-to-cash-flow ratios — in effect, value stocks and value-based mutual funds.

This study also showed that the worst strategy was to buy the trendiest stocks of the moment. These stocks tend to trade at the highest price-to-earnings ratios. The big exception to the rule is small-cap stocks, but these should be considered as only part of an overall portfolio mix and investment strategy.

Other factors to consider in reviewing your RRSP portfolio:

The fund manager. How long has he or she been managing the fund? This is important in the case of a fund with a fairly long track record of outstanding returns. If the manager responsible for these returns has moved on, should you?

Fund size. There is a view that it's very difficult for big funds — funds with assets of $1 billion or more under administration — to stay nimble in the marketplace. The question for us, as investors, is whether size affects performance. In my view, that depends on the fund and its investment philosophy — something you should review on a fund-by-fund basis with your financial adviser.

Portfolio turnover. As a rule, the more a fund trades, the higher the transaction costs. In a lacklustre stock market, that could prove costly. Studies in the U.S. show that low-turnover funds consistently outperform funds that actively trade their portfolios.

Portfolio mix. A diversified portfolio not only helps you spread risk but also reduces volatility. To do that, it's important to hold a mix of funds that do not all go up or down at the same time. That can sometimes happen, quite unintentionally, when investors run after yesterday's hot funds and add what is, in effect, a look-alike to their portfolios.

How many funds are enough? Not an idle question. Many investors fall in love with ideas — and that includes that latest fund concept. There's always a new batch every year — so keep your diversification tendencies in rein.

I personally limit my holdings to eight funds: three equity funds — a value fund, a growth fund, and a small-cap fund; a dividend/income fund; a Canadian bond fund; a U.S. equity fund; and an international emerging-markets fund.

This is all the diversification most of us will ever need. There is no hard-and-fast formula for how much of this fund or that we should have. The amount of risk we can stomach when things go bad in the stock market — and they will — really depends on our circumstances: our investment horizon and, above all, our comfort level.

Bottom line: Develop a custom portfolio that meets your special needs, including the rate of return you'll need to meet your retirement goals. Above all, take the time to sit down with your financial adviser. Develop a portfolio strategy that works for you and meets your retirement goals. Not just this year or the next. But the year after that.

RRSP planning:
More at stake than just tax deductions

RRSPs should be the core of your retirement plan — and that requires time, patience, and, above all, planning. Retirement is, after all, what RRSPs are all about. The actions you take today will have a direct bearing on how you'll live out your retirement years, whether you'll have enough money to travel and do all the things you dream about today — if you had the money and the time.

So, instead of rushing out next February 28 and investing in the first thing that comes to mind, take the time now to sit down with an independent financial adviser — someone who's not married to one company's products or any one institution — and develop a plan and a strategy that reflect your financial needs, your risk tolerance, and your investment horizon.

I suggest now, rather than later, while RRSPs are still fresh in your mind and while you and your adviser have the time to develop a strategy that will work for you and your retirement plans.

Here are a few things you might consider:

* If you have the money, think about making your contribution as soon as possible every year. Now that Ottawa has announced plans to revamp the Canada Pension Plan, who knows how that will impact on your RRSP contribution limits?

* If you have not taken full advantage of any unused RRSP contribution room, think about that, too. It's just too tempting a target to be left alone indefinitely.

* Use the tax savings generated by this year's RRSP to contribute to your RRSP for next year.

* If you have not already done so, consider a life insurance program to protect your RRSP assets from the tax collector in the event of your death.

* Undertake a careful review of your RRSP portfolio to ensure that the asset allocation will produce the returns you'll need for your retirement. That includes maximizing the 20% allowable foreign-content limit. Foreign markets regularly outperform Canadian markets and can make a significant contribution to your portfolio's overall returns.

* If you borrowed to make this year's RRSP contribution, use the tax savings to pay down your loan and channel this payment into next year's RRSP.

* Give serious thought to a monthly savings plan. It's a fantastic way to save and can be used as a tax deduction at source.

Ideally, make your RRSP contribution before next January — if only to avoid being hit with another major obligation right after Christmas. Doing it before makes it easier. A lot easier.

12 steps to a winning RRSP

The 12 steps to creating a winning RRSP are simple. And they work. Ironically, there are also a lot of myths surrounding RRSPs that are either misleading or downright incorrect. Let's first of all deal with what's simple — steps that any of us can take to ensure a comfortable retirement.

Step One: Develop an investment plan that makes sense to you — one that reflects your risk tolerance and investment goals. Above all, an investment plan that will keep you on track when the going gets rough.

Step Two: Choose a financial adviser to help you through the process, especially over the rough spots. There's plenty of evidence to show that investors who make use of an investment professional tend to do better than do-it-yourselfers. A good financial planner will not only help you design a balanced portfolio but also develop a financial plan to maximize your investment strategies.

Step Three: Start early. The earlier the better. The sooner you start, the more you'll have in your retirement kitty. The magic of compounding will do the rest.

Step Four: Maximize your contribution. You'll not only get a tax deduction up front, but your contribution will also start earning tax-sheltered income right away.

Step Five: If you don't have the money, borrow it to maximize your contribution. The tax deduction on the contribution can be used to pay down your loan, and the interest cost on the loan — even though it cannot be used as a tax deduction —

will be more than offset by the compounded returns produced by your contribution. If you've still got unused contribution room, think about borrowing for that, too. The math works in your favour.

Step Six: Develop a balanced portfolio geared to your special requirements. Ideally, it should do two things — it should be designed with your specific risk tolerance in mind, and the portfolio mix should not only produce the level of returns you'll need for your retirement but also do so with reduced volatility. In choosing funds, work closely with your financial adviser to review their performance and whether they reflect your risk profile. We've just gone through two good years in the stock market — so the performance numbers you see advertised may not be reflective of a fund's real performance going forward.

Step Seven: Diversify your risk by investing not only by asset class but internationally as well. As markets go, Canada is small potatoes, and tremendous opportunities await us, as investors, in the global marketplace.

Step Eight: Ignore the day-to-day fluctuation in the marketplace. Take a long-term view, and don't get rattled by sudden upheavals. Market cycles come and go and take time to run their course.

If you want the kind of returns you can brag about, you must be patient. And don't run after the latest hot performer. Studies show that the difference in returns between top performers and the worst in any given year may be very little over a 10-year period.

On a more general level, numerous studies show that you can reduce or almost eliminate the risk of loss by staying invested. A study by Montreal money manager Patrick Forrett, which analyzed the returns of the TSE over 40 years, showed that over one-year periods, the poorest return was -26%; the best, 45%; and the average return, 11%. This study also showed that the longer you hold an investment, the lower the risk. Over five-year periods, for example, the worst return was 0%; the best, a compounded annual return of 25%; and the average, 11% a year.

Step Nine: Review your investment strategies and goals on a regular basis. Circumstances change, and so do our responsibilities. Make sure your financial plan and your investment goals reflect these changes.

Step Ten: Above all, don't procrastinate. The cost of delaying starting your RRSP for even three or four years — or just missing contributions for a couple of years — can be quite staggering 25 or 30 years later.

Step Eleven: Keep your eyes fixed on the future — where you want to be 10, 20, or 30 years from now. Don't be caught up in the swirl of the moment. Develop a plan that will keep you on track no matter what happens in the market this year or next. You'll get there a lot more quickly if you do.

Step Twelve: Know yourself. The best-laid plans of mice and men can fall apart if you confuse what you want with your ability to stay on course during unsteady times. Believe in your future and in yourself.

Should you borrow to contribute to your RRSP?

If you don't have the cash to contribute to your RRSP, you most definitely should. In fact, you should also seriously consider borrowing to use up any contribution room you may have. You can't afford not to.

Suppose you are able to contribute $5,000 this year and you borrow the money to make the contribution. When you put the $5,000 inside your RRSP, you'll get back $2,000 to $2,500, depending on your tax rate. If you use this rebate to pay down your loan, you'll be able to cut the principal virtually in half and your interest cost to about $150 for the year. At the same time, that $5,000 inside your RRSP is working for you, and if it earns 5% or 10%, which is not unreasonable, that works out to $250 to $500 — two or three times your interest cost.

Where else can you double or triple your money? How else can you buy mutual funds and get back close to half your money up front? Another classic example of multi-dimensional investing and how it can tip the scales in your favour.

Note that the interest on the RRSP loan is not tax deductible. But we can easily make it so. Suppose you have $5,000 worth of Canada Savings Bonds, term deposits, or GICs coming up for renewal, or stocks and mutual funds that are redeemable at a profit. If you cash in that $5,000, you know you have $5,000 to put in your RRSP. You'll get a tax rebate of $2,000 or $2,500 right off the bat. You can take this rebate and invest it outside your RRSP.

Better approach: Borrow $5,000 to buy back your investments — or different ones, for that matter. By borrowing to buy investments outside your RRSP, you've just made the interest cost on that loan tax deductible. You'll get a tax rebate of $2,000 or $2,500 in this case, too, which can be used to pay down the loan or, better still, against another loan that is not tax deductible. This will save you non-tax-deductible interest on one side and tax-deductible interest on the other. Another great multi-dimensional win.

Where you can really win bigtime, however, is if you've been accumulating unused carry-forward RRSP room. If you have some investments which have done exceptionally well, think about selling these investments and investing the proceeds inside your RRSP as part of your RRSP catch-up. You could also use proceeds from an inheritance this way.

If you were to use this strategy with, say, $25,000, you'd get back $12,000 in tax rebates, which could be used to pay down non-tax-deductible debt. Also, by continuing to make the same payments on the amount of the loan still outstanding, you'd be able to pay down the remaining principal that much more quickly.

Here, too, I would consider borrowing $25,000 to buy back the same or different investments outside my RRSP. That $25,000 loan now becomes tax deductible — so that your interest cost effectively gets cut in half. In this scenario, you've been able to add $25,000 to your RRSP and pay down non-tax-deductible debt by $12,000.

Bottom line: Make multi-dimensional thinking part of your investment philosophy. It's far, far better than just sitting there and hoping for the best. Every time I think about this, I'm reminded about what Mark Twain had to say on the subject: *"Even if you're on the right track, you'll get run over if you just sit there."*

Spousal RRSPs don't always make sense

It isn't always advantageous to have the higher-income spouse automatically contribute to the other's RRSP. In fact, it could work against you down the road. Your spouse may be in a lower tax bracket today, but that may not be the case a few years from now when you'd like to withdraw some of that money.

He or she may be in line for a monster inheritance. Or own a lot of investments — real estate, mutual funds, stocks, bonds, etc. — that might produce much more income 10 or 15 years from now than you could ever possibly hope to earn. Or you may have no pension where you work, while your spouse has a very good one.

Who knows what the future may hold? But if you believe your spouse will stay employed at the same company, will continue to enjoy great benefits, you're probably better off putting the money into your own RRSP. It requires a bit of guesswork, but part of your long-term strategy should include trying to figure out who will be in the lower tax bracket when it comes time to remove the money.

There are a few other considerations. Perhaps you'll start a business a few years from now. If so, your income will fall, and your tax deductions will increase. You may want to withdraw some of your RRSP at that time. The name of the game is to do so — and to pay little or no tax on the proceeds. All money removed from an RRSP, it should be noted, is effectively taxed as normal income. That means, at your marginal rates.

Even before then, you'd be required to pay a withholding tax on this money. Think about it as a down payment on the tax you'll be expected to pay when you file your income tax return — if the amount is still outside your RRSP when the end of the year rolls around.

It's also worth noting that withholding taxes also rise with the amount you withdraw — 10% on the first $5,000; 20% between $5,000 and $15,000; and 30% on amounts above $15,000. Too many taxpayers remove money from their RRSPs to pay down their mortgages, buy houses, take vacations, or pay other expenses because they think they only have to pay the 10% withholding tax. Come tax time, they find out the hard way.

If, after all these considerations, you find you're better off contributing to a spousal RRSP, you must do so before the end of the RRSP season — February 28 this year — although ideally you'll have far more flexibility if you do so before the end of the year.

So will your spouse. Money contributed by December 31, 1997, for example, can be removed and taxed at your spouse's lower tax rate after December 31, 1999. That's two years, not the normal three years the money must be held in a spousal RRSP. Otherwise, withdrawals are taxed at the contributor's marginal rates.

As a rule, spousal RRSPs do make great sense while you're working and even more when you retire, and they should figure prominently in your retirement planning. They're an especially effective income-splitting tool if you have a significantly higher income or a better corporate pension than your spouse. Under existing rules, you can contribute to your spouse's RRSP — up to your contribution limit — every year to help him or her build up a pension while cutting your taxes in the process.

Name a beneficiary. It's important. If you designate your spouse as your RRSP beneficiary, the assets can be transferred to him or her untaxed. Otherwise, the market value of your RRSP assets will be included as part of your estate and taxed accordingly.

You can, of course, designate another individual as your beneficiary, but other people do not qualify for tax-free rollovers.

As a rule, RRSP/RRIF designations should also be restated in your will and reviewed if there have been any changes in your life. That could be especially important in the case of divorce. Divorce automatically revokes designations in a will.

What to put in your RRSP

People are constantly asking me the kind of investments they should put inside their RRSPs. In today's low interest rate environment, it really doesn't make a difference. The same investment you have outside your RRSP can be put inside your RRSP.

That was not always the case. Investment strategies in the 1960s called for putting interest-bearing investments inside your RRSP — because outside the interest would be fully taxable — and dividend-paying investments outside in order to take full advantage of the dividend tax credit or capital gains deduction.

This theory worked well as long as interest rates were high. Today these yields are no longer there — so compare the yield on your fixed-income investments with the dividend tax credit and capital gains available on equity investments. Term deposits that return 6% a year will double your money every 12 years. A quality mutual fund should double in value every four or five years.

A 40-year-old, for example, who has $10,000 in interest-bearing investments inside her RRSP will have $20,000 at age 52 and $40,000 by age 64.

The same person who invests $10,000 in a mutual fund which doubles every five years will have $20,000 by age 45; $40,000 by age 50; $80,000 by age 55; $160,000 by age 60; and $320,000 by age 65.

Even at a glance, it's pretty clear — **put mutual funds inside your RRSP, dividends and all, if the yield is substantially higher than what you can earn on interest-paying investments.**

At the same time, never reverse the 1960s strategy. Never put interest-bearing investments outside your RRSP. Stocks and mutual funds are fine, however, as long as they offer a higher return, for example, than GICs.

The old argument also goes that if you forgo that dividend tax credit and capital gains deduction by putting these investments inside your RRSP, you'll pay higher taxes when the money is withdrawn.

Just so. Even if you collapse the entire RRSP and have to pay tax on the full $320,000, you'll still have $160,000 at the end of the day. That's four times what fixed-income investments would return during the same period. Even then, after collapsing your $40,000 RRSP, you'll wind up with only $20,000 after taxes. In my books, $160,000 is a lot better than $20,000. Bottom line — change with the times. Otherwise, you're not going to have the standard of living you hope to have in retirement.

Self-directed RRSPs:
Worth the price and then some

Who should have a self-directed RRSP? Everyone. Absolutely no question about it — particularly if you place importance on flexibility and if control over your investments is important to you.

For many investors, the big stumbling block is the annual fee, usually $100 or so. Some (but not all) institutions will waive this fee for a year, or even indefinitely. As in all things, know what you're getting for your money. In my view, the price tag is worth it — and then some — in terms of the choice of investments you can put into your RRSP, and for the superior growth and income potential these investments may offer. With self-directed plans, your investment choices are considerably wider — mutual funds, stocks, bonds, Canada Savings Bonds, GICs, mortgages, mortgage-backed securities, money market funds, and term deposits. Many of these offer significantly higher returns than GICs, for example, and a wider menu to choose from.

And that, in a nutshell, is the real cost. Not the $100 or so annual fee — but the difference between what an alternative investment might have earned, for example, and what a GIC would earn.

Mortgage-backed securities are a good illustration. Term deposit investors, for example, earn a lower rate than those who invest in mortgages and mortgage-backed securities. The latter are how financial institutions earn their money. They take money from us in term deposits, say at 6%, and lend it out as a mortgage at 8.5% to someone else. The difference — the 2.5% your money might have earned elsewhere — is the real fee.

Suppose you had a $10,000 RRSP invested in GICs that returned 6% or $600 a year. Compare this with a blue-chip dividend fund that averaged 10.5% or $1050 a year.

Many self-directed plans cost about $100 a year. At one time, these fees were tax deductible. They no longer are, of course, thanks to the 1996 budget. Ottawa has now decided it will not impose a tax on any funds withdrawn from an RRSP to pay this fee. As a result, many RRSP holders now pay the fee from within their plans. In effect, this represents a tax-free withdrawal from their RRSP.

With an investment of $100,000, of course, the $100 fee is negligible — even more so if the investments inside the self-directed plan earned 2% or 3% more.

Another factor to consider: If you hold a number of mutual funds as part of your RRSP, each may have a trustee fee attached to it. A self-directed RRSP eliminates this problem by consolidating all the funds under a single plan — still with only a single fee. Also, consolidation eliminates the pressure and time loss involved in transferring RRSP funds from one trustee to another to take advantage of a better interest rate or another investment option.

Ask your financial adviser what you're paying in trustee fees and whether you're better off with a self-directed plan. In most cases, you are.

Self-directed RRSPs offer four big advantages:

* They enable investors to consolidate all their investments under one plan.

* They offer a wider choice of investments and greater opportunities for diversification.

* They provide tremendous flexibility, including:

    In-kind contributions — investments do not need to be in cash; investments outside your RRSP can be used as a contribution.
    Conversions — switches from one mutual fund to another or from a maturing GIC, for example, to a stock or a mutual fund.
    Swaps — investments outside your RRSP can be exchanged for investments inside, providing they are eligible and of equal value.

* They offer a handle on foreign content. The allowable percentage of foreign content — currently 20% — in a self-directed

plan is calculated on the book value or cost of applicable investments held.

A self-directed plan enables you to maximize your exposure to markets outside Canada by consolidating them under one plan.

Mutual funds or your RRSP?

It's not really a question of whether you invest in one or the other. It's how you can do both. Best strategy — put your money into your RRSP, using it to buy mutual funds. This way, you'll get the best of both worlds — tax relief and an income-producing investment. Ironically, a lot of people seem confused by this. They shouldn't be, as a little number crunching will quickly show.

Here's what happens if you're in the 40% tax bracket and invest $5,000 outside an RRSP and the same money inside an RRSP.

First of all, outside your RRSP, you'll lose $2,000 of your $5,000 investment in taxes. That represents a 40% loss before you even start. If the remaining $3,000 earns 10% or $300, you'll lose another $120 in taxes. Bottom line at the end of the year — your investment will now be worth $3,180 after taxes.

Inside your RRSP, the $5,000 will retain its value and, if it also earns 10%, it will be worth $5,500 at the end of the year. The difference — $2,320. That's why you should always exhaust every tax deduction you can before considering investments outside your RRSP.

Match your RRSP — good for seniors, too

Double the value of your RRSP in one day? Absolutely — through the "match your RRSP plan" offered by some independent financial planners. It's a simple process, and it's stunningly successful when used properly.

If you contribute to your RRSP, you're not allowed to use it as collateral for a loan. If you do, and Revenue Canada finds out, it will deregister your plan and make it fully taxable. The "match your RRSP plan" gets around this very neatly.

If you invest $5,000, for example, with an independent financial planner, he or she will arrange for you to borrow an equal amount outside your RRSP. These funds can then be used to buy foreign investments which have historically outperformed many investments Canadian taxpayers keep inside their RRSPs.

Also, because this investment is outside your RRSP, the interest is tax deductible — and because the initial $5,000 is inside your RRSP, you'll get back at least $2,000 from Ottawa as a tax rebate. This means you'll only have $3,000 of your own money invested.

At 10%, the $10,000 will earn $1,000 a year. That represents a 33.33% return on the $3,000. How many people earn that much on their RRSP?

That $3,000 is a loan. You don't have to mortgage your home to get it. And, as I noted earlier, you can pledge non-RRSP investments, although you can't pledge your RRSP as collateral. The lending institution will simply hold the mutual funds you buy outside your RRSP until the $3,000 is repaid.

This can be a very effective strategy to build up your retirement capital — but it also takes time. If your time horizon is short, or there is a real possibility you will need to pay off the loan in the near future, or you have difficulty in weathering the ups and downs of the market, this may not be an option for you. However, if you can take these storms in your stride and are prepared to hold your investment for at least five years, this plan should produce the kind of returns you expect.

Used prudently, this plan can also work well for seniors who are about to face some pretty big tax hits down the road. Ottawa is desperately short of money. It already claws back the Old Age Security, and rumours abound about the Canada Pension Plan and other social benefits.

In addition, many seniors will be hurt by the cancellation of the right to contribute up to $6,000 of work-related pension into a spousal RRSP. Seniors who have accumulated a large amount of money inside their RRSPs can use this strategy to manufacture a tax deduction similar to what they would get by contributing to an RRSP.

Let's say you have $100,000 inside your RRSP and arrange with your financial planner to match it with an investment outside your plan. The interest on that loan — usually prime plus 1% — would amount to about $8,250 a year. Because the loan was used to purchase investments outside your RRSP, this interest is tax deductible.

Best of all for seniors, **the $8,250 appears as a tax deduction before the net income line that determines whether your Old Age Security is clawed back.**

Another point to keep in mind: It's not just a matter of matching what you put in. You can also match what's already in your RRSP. If you have $100,000 inside your RRSP, for example, you can match it with $100,000 outside. Let's say you borrow that money at 6%. Annual interest charges will amount to $6,000, which is tax deductible against any form of income you have, including withdrawals from your RRSP or RRIF. These withdrawals are taxable, of course, but the tax deductions would wipe out the tax on this removal.

This is a simple way to get money out of your RRSP tax-free and effectively transfer it to an investment portfolio that does not require you to withdraw money on an annual basis, as you must in the case of RRIFs. There's no age 69 with investments.

Net result: You pay little or nothing in real cost because of the tax relief and because you'll still be able to retain OAS benefits. Plus, and this is not insignificant, the profits generated by these investments will more than make up for any tax considerations. That's the kind of trade-off I really like.

Foreign content: Don't play too close to the line

Many investors who run the foreign content in their RRSPs close to the 20% mark could easily find themselves out of balance for part of the year. Especially if they hold Templeton Growth, which distributes dividends in midyear. Most funds do so at the end of the year.

When this happens — most often in the case of locked-in RRSPs where no further contributions are made — the RRSP is out of balance for six months and then, when Canadian funds make their distributions, goes back into balance for the rest of the year. There is a cost, albeit a small one, whenever this happens — a penalty of 1% for every month your RRSP is over the allowable limit. The penalty is levied on the amount over this limit.

Many of the problems with foreign content are largely the result of investor misunderstanding of the rules governing foreign content, particularly how to value the foreign assets in their plans.

The 20% limit is based on the book value or the original purchase price of the funds in your RRSP — not on their current market value. So far, so good. But the water can get a bit muddied when you transfer foreign RRSP assets from one financial institution to another. If the funds are transferred on an individual basis, some institutions will value these assets at their current market value — not at their original book value. This can immediately put your foreign content over the 20% limit. Much depends on the institution making the transfer — whether it provides all relevant information, particularly the original acquisition costs of the foreign assets.

That's one of the advantages of a self-directed RRSP. If the plan is transferred in whole from one institution to another, the book value of your plan's foreign assets will not be affected.

Be careful, though. That protection does not extend to the transfer of individual funds. To avoid this complication, make sure you transfer your entire RRSP holdings at one time. To be on the safe side, keep all documentation that can provide the book value of your RRSP assets.

Other problems arise if you decide to sell one of the foreign funds inside your RRSP and use the proceeds to acquire another foreign investment. If the original fund has risen in value more than the Canadian funds over the period, the transaction could put your foreign content out of whack. It can also be thrown out of balance by something as simple as redeeming units to pay self-directed trustee fees.

The simplest way to avoid these complications is to limit your foreign content to 17% or 18% and to be acutely aware of what can happen to the book value of your RRSP holdings every time you change funds, make subsequent purchases inside your RRSP, or transfer your RRSP to another financial institution.

It's time to drop the "R" from RRSPs

When Ottawa invented the Registered Retirement Savings Plan, or RRSP, it did investors a terrible disservice — not in creating but in naming RRSPs.

Dropping the second "R" would be more to the point. By calling them "retirement" plans, Ottawa has firmly put in our heads the idea that the RRSP is a savings vehicle to help us put aside money for our retirement. That's certainly true, but in the process, it has turned off thousands of young Canadians who either don't want to think about retirement or who believe that day may never come.

Ironically, older Canadians who are at or near retirement also shy away from RRSPs because they feel they're already there. Once they reach retirement, they feel their savings could be put to much better use, namely supplementing their reduced standard of living.

I'd like to see the second "R" removed from these plans and have them called Registered Savings Plans or RSPs instead. Admittedly, the name lacks pizzazz, but it's not a turnoff either. A better translation might be Rebate Savings Plan — a savings program you put money into and save taxes. And like current RRSPs, all earnings inside the plan would compound tax-free until you decide to remove that money. At that time, as has been noted elsewhere in this chapter, any money withdrawn is taxed at your marginal tax rate. However, if you have no taxable income, you will pay no tax or very little, depending on the amount you withdraw.

Keep in mind that you are not required to keep contributions inside your RRSP until you retire. Under current tax rules, RRSP contributions do not have to be held for more than one day to qualify as a tax deduction. If we think of RRSPs as simply a way to help us save taxes, I'm sure more people would make use of them. Everyone, in fact, who has not turned 70 and who has taxable income should use an RRSP as the cornerstone of his or her retirement plan.

Without question, these plans are best for younger savers, who benefit far, far more from the long-term advantages of tax-free compounding. A 25-year-old, for example, who contributes $3,000 a year to an RRSP that earns 9% annually would accumulate $1.1 million by her 65th birthday.

If the same individual waits until age 30 to start — that is, contributing the same amount every year — she would have only $705,373 at age 65. The difference in cost to her is only $15,000, yet that $400,000 difference in return would easily produce a lifetime income of $40,000 a year. That's precisely what waiting five years costs your retirement.

The reason for this big gap is that you not only receive a tax deduction when you contribute the money, but it also grows completely tax-free inside the plan as long as it remains there.

That brings up another important point — the rate of return you earn on your contributions. A 30-year-old, for example, who puts $1,000 a year outside his RRSP in a GIC that earns 8% a year will accumulate $40,000 by age 65. The same amount contributed for the same number of years in an RRSP and earning the same rate of return would grow to $185,000.

The same amount of money, the same length of time, the same rate of return. The only difference — the second savings plan has an "R" in front of it.

If you can improve on that 8% return — and many dividend funds produce average compound annual returns in the order of 10% — without exposing yourself to undue risk, the result can make a huge difference in your retirement lifestyle. A 12% return in this example would grow to $485,000 by the time you reach 65 — that's $300,000 more than you would get with an 8% return.

Don't qualify for an RRSP?

If you don't qualify for an RRSP, there is a way to force one. If you're retired, for example, and live off investment income, you probably already know that this type of investment income does not qualify as earned income for RRSP purposes.

One thing you can do is make an investment in rental real estate — one that will produce positive cash flow and earnings. You get a double advantage here. First, the interest on the loan to purchase the property is a tax-deductible expense. Second, the maintenance — utilities, insurance, property taxes, etc. — is deductible as well. These will wipe out most of the taxable income from the investment.

What's left over is classed as earned income for RRSP purposes — the only type of investment income, by the way, that's considered earned income for RRSP contributions.

Locking in RRSP profits

With stock markets and mutual funds enjoying seven years of unparallelled success, you may be wondering whether it's time to take some profits, especially if these investments are inside your RRSP.

The only fly in the ointment is that you can't get tax relief on any losers inside your plan. This is a growing concern for many Canadians who feel the market may be getting top-heavy. At least, when you sell outside, you get capital gains deductions that can be used to wipe out the capital gains taxes on other profitable investments.

Of course, if you've been in the market for the past few years, you really don't have to worry a lot about losses. If you're like most people, your biggest concern is how to conserve what you've already made — without having to sell and trigger a big capital gain.

There is a way to handle this which you may find useful.

Before getting into that, though, I'd like to stress that I'm a great fan of buying top-quality stocks and mutual funds and hanging on, especially if the investments are outside my RRSP. One of the reasons is that when you sell, you have to share your profits with the tax collector. As a result, you have less to reinvest. If your investments have done well inside your RRSP — and you would like to take some profits — you can sell, go short-term, and reinvest when prices are lower.

However, if you would like to hang on to these investments, but don't like the idea of parting with investments that won't give you a capital loss, you may find this strategy useful: If you have cash outside your RRSP, think about using it to buy some of the more profitable investments from inside your RRSP. Keep in mind that you can sell any investments inside your RRSP anytime you want. That includes selling them to yourself and holding them outside your RRSP.

This strategy will enable you to lock a tax-free capital gain inside your RRSP and provide you with the cash to buy other investments for your RRSP, or you can wait until the market corrects. In addition, you now own the investments outside your RRSP. This puts you in a position to ride your profits all the way and have them taxed as capital gains when you sell. Or if the market corrects, you can sell them and trigger a capital loss to offset some of your other capital gains.

Later, when you think the markets are going to recover, you can use the cash inside your RRSP to make new investments — or even the same investments you had before — only at a lower base price.

Bottom line: Selling investments out of your RRSP can create some handsome tax relief in addition to the normal deductions for contributing to your RRSP.

What about withdrawing money from your RRSP under the Home Ownership Plan?

Under the Home Ownership Plan, first-time homeowners are able to borrow up to $20,000 from their RRSPs to put against the purchase of a home. That's per person — a couple can borrow up to $40,000. The money must be repaid over a 15-year period.

I'm not really a big fan of this program. I see it as little more than a last resort to be used only if you're having trouble getting enough money together to buy a home.

I'm all for buying a home — even if it means borrowing from your RRSP if there's no other way — but most of us would be better off exhausting all other options before deciding on this course.

First, if you fail to make repayments on time, the amount is considered a withdrawal from your RRSP and added to your income for that year and taxed accordingly. In addition, missed repayments cannot be put back later.

Second — and perhaps most important — you'll lose growth in your RRSP. Mutual funds have outperformed real estate by a wide margin during the past 30 years. By cashing in these investments to get enough money together to buy a home, you're also stunting the growth of your RRSP.

You'd be far better off tacking that $20,000 onto your mortgage rather than lending the money to yourself out of your RRSP at zero interest. And under no circumstances should you ever cash in your RRSP to pay down your mortgage. If you do, you'll lose 40% to 50% of it to the tax collector. Compare that with what you'd save on the extra $20,000 on your mortgage — 6% or 7%. It doesn't make mathematical sense.

If you're selling your home and the purchaser demands a vendor take-back mortgage (the seller offers a mortgage to the buyer) as part of the deal, you should understand this is double jeopardy, as far as you're concerned. First, you don't get the $50,000 you expected, for example, to put toward the purchase of your new home, which means you have to finance a $50,000-bigger mortgage. Second, the interest on that new mortgage is not tax deductible — but the interest you earn on the vendor take-back mortgage is.

Better option: Under current rules, your RRSP is allowed to invest in mortgages on Canadian property. If the property does not belong to you, the mortgage does not need to be insured. Your RRSP then lends the buyer the money and earns interest on the mortgage tax-free. And you'll have the extra $50,000 you counted on to put against your new mortgage.

By using this strategy, you'll be able to move $50,000 out of your RRSP tax-free to purchase your new home — a win-win multi-dimensional saving for you — perhaps even triple — and the purchaser ends up with a one-year loan (you really don't want to go beyond this) and time to arrange other financing.

Chapter 3

Investment Strategies That Can Work for You

If money doesn't grow on trees,
why do banks have so many branches?

First rule of investing — know yourself

With the fear of a major sell-off always hanging over our heads, there's an enormous temptation to wait it out on the sidelines — at least until the worst appears to be over.

   The problem with this strategy is that we don't know when the sell-off will start or when the market will turn up again. That's crucial in an area where timing is everything. By sitting it out too early, we risk missing out on some of the biggest gains before the market drops or when it takes off again, often without warning.

The record for investors who try to second-guess the market is dismal, and there's plenty of folklore to make this point over and over.

Peter Lynch, who guided the fortunes of Fidelity's flagship Magellan Fund, produced returns of 20% every year for 10 years. If you stayed with the fund, good markets and bad, your investment would have quadrupled over the period. Interestingly, investors who bought his fund and tried to time the market during this 10-year period actually lost about 1% a year.

Mackenzie Financial makes the same point, comparing the returns of an investor who bought and held its Industrial Growth Fund for 25 years to an investor who switched to the latest "hot" Canadian equity fund every year. Here's what would have happened if you had invested $10,000 in Mackenzie's Growth Fund in December 1974 — that $10,000 would have grown by 1,786%, or to $178,622, by June 1997. In comparison, if you had switched to the latest "hot" equity fund — the one that produced the highest 12-month return every year — your $10,000 would have grown to $131,768, assuming you had been able to switch without fees, and to $81,140 if switching fees had been charged.

Statistics, in fact, show that only 25% of each year's "hot" funds make it to the first quartile in the following year. About 25% slip to the second quartile; 20% more end up as third quartile performers; and the final 30% end up in the fourth quartile.

If you had tried to time the market — and missed being in the Industrial Growth Fund during the market's 10 best months over the 25-year period, the $10,000 would have grown to $109,200 — some $196,000 less than if you had just invested the $10,000 in Industrial Growth Fund and forgot about it for 25 years.

There are plenty of other examples, and they all make the same point: The ultimate value of your investment has little to do with the rate of return you earn. It has everything to do with the compounding rate of return. If you're not in the market during the market's "best" times — and there's no way to forecast these — you won't have these gains to compound.

The bottom line is that you've got to be there. Not just in good markets but also in down markets. If you don't go out in the boat, you can't catch the fish.

What does it take to save $1 million?

Very little. Or a lot. It depends when you start.

Most people think it's a question of yield. I'm afraid it's not. It's time — and the magic of compounding.

If you're a 30-year-old, for example, and you contribute $3,000 a year to your RRSP, which earns an average of 9% a year for the next 35 years, you'll have $705,373 by the time you're age 65.

If you started just five years earlier — at age 25 — and put the same amount in your RRSP every year, you'd have $1.1 million when you reach 65.

So how much does it cost to have over $1 million at age 65? The cost is $68,000 — $120,000 in contributions less $52,000 in tax rebates over the 40-year period.

A 30-year-old who invests $5,000 a year ($3,250 after tax rebates) would have $133,000 less at age 65. Again, a pretty graphic example of the magic of compounding.

Let's reverse it. If your goal is to have $1 million by the time you reach 60, how much do you need to invest every year to make this happen?

First, pick a reasonable rate of return — say 13% a year (that's less than a good-performing mutual fund) — and the number of years before you reach 60. At age 25, you require just $118 a month; at age 30, the amount goes to $225 a month; and at age 35, you'll need $445 a month. If you're 40, your monthly investment will go up to $882; and at age 45, almost $1,820 a month.

Obviously, the earlier you start, the better — but how do you convince a 25-year-old to put away $118 a month?

Let's look at it another way. Say you can invest $500 a month and can earn 13% on that investment. If you're 55 and still plan to retire when you're 60, that $500 a month will produce $42,000. If you begin at age 50, your investment will grow to $122,000; at age 45, to $275,000; at 40, to $567,000; at 35, to $1,235,000; at 30, $2,186,000; and at 25, to $4,250,000.

Given the current global outlook — and trends — there's no question that younger people should have a high percentage of their money inside a mutual fund and as high a percentage as possible in foreign funds.

Before leaving this, it's worth noting that a $1,000-a-year RRSP begun at age 25 will accumulate more by the time you're 60 than $3,000 invested every year beginning at age 40. It's not the rate. It's the time.

Load or no-load?

As a rule, I don't believe you should buy mutual funds yourself — simply because I think you're not going to get objective advice.

If you call a bank or trust company and ask whether you should buy its funds, what do you think it will tell you? If you ask whether the time has come for you to sell its funds, what do you think it will tell you? Banks and trust companies are not objective — they're tied to one product line and only that line.

The value of having an independent financial planner between you and whatever financial product you're buying is that independent financial planners have to be objective. They're working for you. *Not* for the financial institution which is offering the investment.

They may have a decided bias toward mutual funds, or even some other form of investment, but at the end of the day there's going to be a finder's fee — no matter what.

Mind you, you can escape paying a load or sales commission when you buy certain funds. No-load funds can be purchased without a sales commission. Most load funds, however, also offer the option of rear-end loads, which enable investors to pay the loads only when they sell. This option also makes more money available to work for you from Day One. And, best of all, if you hold the fund for seven years or so, you won't have to pay any load at all.

That's why many investment companies have created fund families, which enable you to move your investment from a bond fund, for example, to a balanced fund or an equity fund — usually at no charge. The trick is to invest in a family of funds that you feel comfortable with and that meet your financial objectives.

The cost of bailing out

Asset-strategy consultant Frank Russell, head of one of the world's leading investment-management firms, says investors should think twice before bailing out of the market during periods of correction. Or even making a major change in the asset mix of their portfolios.

There are costs involved with this strategy — beyond the usual commission charges — that investors often overlook and that underline the risks associated with trying to time the market.

In order for this strategy to work, studies conducted by Russell show, there must be some tendency for the market to trend in one direction or another. That, of course, is usually the exception rather than the rule and does not reflect the performance of certain market sectors where there is no discernible consistency.

Outperformance of small caps, for example, has tended to come in large lumps, and any timing strategy may run the risk of missing the next period of outperformance altogether. "While some small-cap strategies may save you wasted time at the dock, they carry with them the possibility of missing the boat altogether," says Russell.

That's why Russell's firm, which pioneered the multi-manager, multi-style concept in investing, has always emphasized a long-term approach to its investment management.

Patience is what successful investing is all about — and a strategy you can live with during unsettling periods in the market. To work best, this strategy should be worked out in what Russell calls "the confident calm" of a rising market rather than in the frantic pressure of a market sell-off.

Russell's studies also show that, on average, equities will likely produce higher returns than bonds. "That means," says Russell, "that any reduction in equity exposure in reaction to disappointing results will likely cost the investor returns. This premium is the cost of bailing out."

In assessing the costs of bailing out, Russell compares the performance of a "disciplined" investor with a portfolio of 60% equities and 40% bonds, which is rebalanced monthly regardless of market environment, with that of an investor with a similar portfolio who bails out during periods of market upheaval, when he or she shifts the asset allocation to 20% equities and 80% bonds. The difference in returns is not only striking but also consistent.

The Russell study concludes: "The one certainty that comes from investing in equities is that we will have periods of disappointment. The best strategy — the disciplined approach — is to stick to the allocation that represents the long-term objectives of the investor. . . ." That applies especially, says Russell, to early withdrawals from your RRSP, which can significantly decrease the amount you'll have to fund your retirement. You may find the overall cost is simply not worth it.

Russell cites the example of a 40-year-old who withdraws $10,000 from his RRSP to buy a home. Immediate cost is a $1,000 early-withdrawal penalty and $2,800 federal income tax on the withdrawal. Total — $3,800.

Assuming this individual contributes 8% of his salary to the company's savings plan, he would accumulate $405,000 at the end of 30 years.

If he withdrew $10,000 after being in the plan for 10 years, his total accumulated savings after 30 years would be $360,000.

Total cost of that $10,000 withdrawal — $45,000 in accumulated savings plus up-front costs of $3,800, or a total of $48,800.

The same argument could be made about bailing out of the market because you think it's about to go down.

The biggest mistake most of us make is adopting spur-of-the-minute, short-term strategies without due regard to our long-term objectives and ultimate results — all of which underline the importance of developing a long-term investment strategy that meets your objectives and risk tolerance.

Mutual fund returns

Ever wonder why your mutual fund didn't produce the returns published by the fund company? There are plenty of reasons, especially if you've been in the fund for four or five years.

The performance figures are based on a buy-and-hold strategy and the reinvestment of all dividends declared by the fund. Obviously, if you take your dividends in cash or withdraw even 10% during a year when the market is down, the long-term effect on your overall returns can be quite dramatic.

Always, always take advantage of sell-offs

A few years ago, when stock markets were struggling to make ends meet, I urged investors to jump in with both feet. Unfortunately, as I noted at the time, stocks are about the only thing people won't buy when they're on sale. Even more so when prices drop by as much as 20% or 30%.

In these cases, emotion takes over from common sense. Yet if these investors had bought, they would have been far better off. By how much? As much as 18% at that time. In comparison, a one-year GIC would have yielded 7.25% over the same period.

Talvest Growth Fund, for example, produced an 18.65% return during this period, while Templeton Growth and Trimark Canadian posted gains of 11% and 11.4% respectively.

In the case of a $20,000 portfolio, this translates to $21,450 for a one-year GIC; $23,720 for Talvest Growth; $22,300 for Templeton Growth; and $22,800 for Trimark Canadian during the period covered.

For investors who opted for GICs at the time, the difference is even more striking. Sixth-month returns for these funds during the same period were about 8.6% for Talvest Growth; 9% for Templeton Growth; and 5.73% for Trimark Canadian. A one-year GIC for the same period would have earned 3.5%.

Your portfolio also needs an annual checkup

Your portfolio's checkup, also called portfolio rebalancing, should be done at least once a year to ensure that your asset mix accurately reflects your investment goals and risk tolerance on an ongoing basis.

The process involves setting targets for different asset classes and sectors within your portfolio — for example, 25% blue-chip equity funds; 25% growth funds; 15% foreign equity funds; 25%

bond funds; and 10% money market funds. Rebalancing will ensure that your portfolio sticks to this asset mix — one that you feel comfortable with and that doesn't expose you to undue risk.

When your portfolio mix gets out of balance, so will the risk-to-reward ratio that works for you.

Before getting into the pros and cons of portfolio balancing, a brief word is in order about strategic asset allocation and the so-called "efficient frontier," one of the current industry buzzwords.

The process involves analyzing your risk tolerance to determine just how much risk you're prepared to take and how much return you can reasonably expect in relation to that risk. Ideally, the asset mix of your portfolio should be constructed to deliver those returns, that is, smoothing out the sudden ups and downs that visit equity and bond markets from time to time.

The reason portfolios get out of balance is that asset classes do not grow at the same rate. If your portfolio mix is 60% equities and 40% bonds, for example, and equities grow at a rate of 16% and bonds at 8%, your asset mix will ultimately get out of whack — with the result that you'll eventually move off the efficient frontier, the asset mix that will deliver the returns you want at a risk level you feel comfortable with.

The efficient frontier, it should be noted, is not a thin line but an area. Even so, if you don't rebalance from time to time, you'll stray off the efficient frontier, getting results that you may not feel comfortable with. Some professionals suggest rebalancing twice a year. For most people, once a year is enough, keeping in mind that your portfolio is a moving target.

The process involves selling off a portion of the overvalued asset or sector and adding to the asset class that has shown the slowest growth. By using this strategy, you'll generally buy an undervalued asset over time.

This is especially important in dollar-cost averaging programs. That's where you invest the same amount — for example, $100 or $200 every month — to acquire shares in a mutual fund. When the fund's units are up, you buy fewer units; when they're down, you're able to buy more.

How effective is rebalancing? U.S. fund manager T. Rowe Price recently compared two rebalancing strategies over a 25-year period. The study looked at two $10,000 portfolios, both of which started with a mix of 60% blue chips, 30% government bonds, and 10% T-Bills.

One portfolio was rebalanced to these target ratios every three months. The other was left to grow unchecked. After 25 years, the rebalanced portfolio grew to $145,000 and the unchecked portfolio to $141,000 — not much difference, but the ride over the 25-year period was a lot smoother and a lot easier.

The results were somewhat different in another study by T. Rowe Price. Here Price looked at two all-equity portfolios of $10,000 each. Both started with 50% blue-chip stocks, 25% small-cap companies, and 25% foreign equities. In this instance, the rebalanced portfolio grew to $244,000 and the unchecked portfolio to $223,000 during the same 25-year period.

If your fund manager leaves, should you leave, too?

Unless there are compelling reasons to the contrary, stay put if your fund manager leaves. Most mutual funds are managed under a certain mandate, and, as long as the mandate doesn't change, there's really no advantage to moving.

Most investors don't realize that portfolio managers have very little latitude in how they manage their funds. In fact, they are instructed to manage the fund in a certain way — within clearly defined parameters.

A case in point is Templeton Growth Fund. Even though Sir John is no longer active in the management of the fund, the new managers continue to follow his precepts and investment philosophy. They may try to make certain enhancements, I understand, but everything else remains the same. Did everyone sell when Sir John stepped down? Not at all. His legacy is still the fund's management style, which lives on whether he's there or not.

The question you should ask yourself as an investor is not whether you liked the manager, but whether you liked the investment style of the fund. If you liked it with the previous manager, you will probably like it with the new management team as well, because the fund will be following essentially the same investment style and strategy that attracted you to it in the first place. All that's really changing is the individual who executes the mandate of the fund.

When Peter Lynch left Fidelity's flagship fund, Magellan, after turning in 20%-plus annual returns over a decade, Fidelity brought in another manager with a similar style. How did he do? He actually had better performance numbers.

Part of the confusion in investors' minds can be laid squarely on the shoulders of the fund companies themselves, which created a star system as part of a marketing strategy to hype the sale of funds. Many of these fund companies have found, as we saw recently with AGF and Fidelity, that this strategy can also backfire.

There are also tax implications. If the fund is outside your RRSP, you may trigger a capital gain. That's not a consideration, of course, if the fund is inside your RRSP.

Another point to keep in mind: Over time, most managers tend toward the mean. Some years, they're big winners; some years, they're not so hot.

At the end of the day, asset selection is more important than choosing the "right" fund manager. The U.S. market, for example, has been much stronger than the Canadian markets during much of the past 10 years. In this environment, a top-notch Canadian manager would have underperformed a really poor U.S. manager.

Bottom line: What matters is not whether there's a change in managers but whether there's a fundamental change in the way the fund is being managed or a new investment approach you may not feel comfortable with.

How long do bear markets last?

An apt question as markets topple one new record after another.

The short answer is bull markets last longer than bear markets, according to a 1995 study by HRC Consultants, which examined 13 U.S. market cycles going back more than 50 years, from April 1942 to April 1994.

The study showed that the average bull market lasted 3.11 years and produced gains of 90.27%, while in comparison bear markets were less than a year in duration — 0.89 of a year to be exact — and the average loss was 25.15%. That's less than one-third of the gains produced in the preceding bull market.

The study underlines the importance of staying invested throughout the market cycle and taking a long-term view in reaching our investment goals. One of the best ways to deal with this is to ignore day-to-day fluctuations in the unit values of your mutual funds.

Market cycles come and go and must be viewed from a long-term perspective. These cycles reflect changes in economic circumstances, the interest rate environment, and other factors that influence stock prices. This is not always easy to remember when markets go into a dizzying tailspin — that corrections do not last forever, that some of the biggest gains produced by equity markets follow in the wake of these downturns.

Another point to keep in mind — and this is something many people forget — when you follow a buy-and-sell strategy, you have to pay taxes on any profits, and these taxes leave you, ironically, with less money to invest.

Risk: It's really a question of time

Of all the words in investing, the most misunderstood — and misused — is "risk." We talk about this mutual fund or that mutual fund being riskier and how to reduce risk by changing the asset mix of our investments. What we're really talking about is whether we can handle volatility — sharp drops in stock prices that visit equity markets from time to time like a bad head cold.

To me, risk is a factor of time. Other than guaranteed fixed-income investments that can be cashed at any time, all others carry a certain element of risk, some more than others — if there is a possibility we may need that money in a few months' time.

There is, in fact, hardly any risk to a good equity-based mutual fund if you hold it for five or more years. Held for five or seven years — the normal course of an economic cycle — a large number of mutual funds will easily produce a compounded rate of return of 8%, 9%, or 10% a year. Some even more.

I know many investors shift from one investment to another in search of better returns, often with undesirable results. In 1993, when growth funds were posting double-digit returns, many GIC investors moved into the market in a big way, only to see their investments fall from grace in 1994, when many of the same funds recorded losses. The result — a switch back to the safety and guarantees of GICs, usually at the lowest point in the market downturn.

In 1995, stock markets again gathered momentum, with New York recording gains in the order of 30% and Canadian markets somewhat less. Canadian markets played catch-up in 1996 and continued to push ahead in 1997, despite a growing unease in most major world markets.

In this environment, many GIC holders are going to look at growth funds again without understanding how stock markets work — that they don't go up forever or down forever — and that if investors hold whatever funds they buy this year for at least five years, they will not only show a good return on their investment, but the returns, in most cases, will also be significantly higher than what they would have earned on GICs. GIC investors who bought into the high-flying market of 1993 would be sitting quite pretty today if they had stayed the course.

If you feel uncomfortable with growth funds, ask your financial adviser about dividend funds or equity funds that focus on blue chips — value stocks that not only pay dividends but are also able to take market downturns in their stride. Whatever the case, you need more than GICs to make it happen.

Create your own deposit insurance

There's a hidden cost to the insurance that guarantees your bank and trust company deposits. Not only do they pay a low rate of interest, but you also get no tax breaks on interest income. That's the cost of restricting your investments to GICs and the like.

The same investment in mutual funds or stocks will not only provide the same or better return but also yield a tax break on any dividends you receive or on any capital gains that result.

It's a trade-off between absolute return of capital — with low yields at full tax — and no guarantees, with the opportunity of 12% or 15% returns with every tax break available.

Suppose you had taken $10,000 20 years ago and invested in Canada Savings Bonds, which averaged 8% over this period — with unlimited guarantees. Your $10,000 would now be worth

$46,609, and in term deposits the same $10,000 would have increased to $67,274.

Why not make your own deposit insurance? You can do this by simply diversifying your investments.

First, you could have split your $10,000 into five individual $2,000 investment units.

Then you could have put the initial $2,000 in a savings account, which averaged 5% a year over that period. In 20 years, the $2,000 would have been worth $5,306.

You could have invested the second $2,000 in a term deposit, which is also guaranteed unconditionally. In 20 years, it would have been worth $13,455.

With the third $2,000, you could have invested in a mutual fund, many of which averaged 15% returns over the period. Here the $2,000 would have grown to $32,733.

You could have invested the fourth $2,000 in an international fund, which averaged returns of 18% — not unusual for this type of investment. This $2,000 would have grown to $54,786.

Now let's assume you had put the final $2,000 in Bre-X and lost it all.

Despite the loss of 20% of your total investment, your original $10,000 would now be worth $106,280 — that's almost $2,000 a year more than just investing in guaranteed term deposits.

That's the real cost of deposit insurance.

RRSPs are not the only game in town

RRSPs aren't the only way to cut your tax bill or save for your retirement. This has always been a concern for many Canadians who don't qualify for an RRSP because of their age or their income mix or because they enjoy a full pension at work.

There are a few ways, however, to save taxes without the restrictions that accompany RRSPs. A good example is real estate.

All interest and operating expenses are tax deductible against rental income and eventually against other forms of income. Also, only 75% of any capital gains is taxable. In comparison, any money removed from your RRSP is taxed at your marginal rate.

Not everybody, however, wants to manage real estate, and the capital involved is often too large for a small investor. Also, real estate prices are cyclical and do not always go up or down in line with either the stock market or the economy. That's important in times of market uncertainty and one of the reasons why real estate may be worth a second look at this point in the real estate cycle, which lasts on average 18 years.

One of the best ways to participate is through a real estate fund, which offers investors the best of all worlds — full liquidity, a chance to ride the cycle from start to finish, and the opportunity to get off anytime you wish.

Another alternative is rental real estate, a prime example of no-lose multi-dimensional investing, which produces a regular flow of real estate income no matter what happens in the stock market. Compare that with an investment in raw land, which produces no income — a situation that can prove both costly and disastrous for owners waiting out a lacklustre market.

Another investment that does not move in sync with the stock market is gold. Best way to hedge your bets: A gold fund, which may hold not only gold bullion but also dividend-paying gold stocks that can produce capital gains, even if gold prices go nowhere in the meantime. Another classic case of making multi-dimensional investing work for you.

Other investors manufacture tax relief by borrowing to buy investments like mutual funds and stocks.

If you can save $200 a month for the next five years, you'll have $2,400 at the end of each year — plus any capital gains and dividends/interest generated by that investment. Instead, think about borrowing $30,000 and using the money to buy mutual funds or blue-chip stocks. At 8%, interest on this loan would amount to $2,400 a year or $200 a month — the same amount as your monthly investment, but this strategy will enable you to manufacture tax savings of $1,000 to $1,200, depending on your tax rate.

In the long run — and that's the key — the $30,000 invested in a blue-chip mutual fund should also produce solid returns over this period. Fifteen years down the road, that $30,000 investment, averaging returns of 10% a year, should be worth $125,300. At that time, you can pay off the loan and pocket the difference of $95,300 — much of it in the form of capital appreciation. After deducting after-tax interest costs of about $1,200 a year, your net gain would be about $77,300.

Tax shelters should be good investments first

Don't let anyone talk you into buying something simply because it offers great tax relief. If it's the tax relief that makes it, then it's generally not a good investment, and if you're smart you'll stay clear.

You want a good investment, first and foremost, because it's the investment you'll have to live with. The tax relief you get is usually a one-shot deal or, at best, something that lasts only a couple of years.

The last thing you need is to put yourself in a position where you buy something simply for tax-planning purposes. The best approach is to have an independent assessor review the investment carefully. If it stands up, then the tax relief is a great bonus.

Next thing: Never buy a limited partnership directly from the individual or individuals who developed it. Do you think they'll ever tell you that theirs is second-best or the worst on the street?

What you want is someone who will give you straight answers, a hard-nosed evaluation, and the kind of tax relief that suits your particular situation.

Limited partnerships, however, can be a godsend to some people — perhaps to most of us at some point in our careers. If you just got a big settlement, for example, or made a big capital gain, or you simply want to start taking money out of your RRSP, a limited partnership that offers tax relief and puts you in a position to take out an equal amount from your RRSP tax-free is fundamentally good financial planning.

At the end of the day, however, limited partnerships must stand alone on their investment merits. That point is very dear to Revenue Canada's heart. In fact, a lot of people who bought limited partnerships in the past found themselves audited and reassessed by Revenue Canada because of this.

If it doesn't have investment merit, it will come back to haunt you sooner or later. Count on it.

Best time to put a limited partnership in place? Historically, December is the big month for limited partnerships — but given the government's options, it's something you might want to think about before any Budget Day.

All of which underline the importance of multi-dimensional investing and ensuring that every investment you make is part of a solid financial plan.

The three main elements of such a strategy are tax planning, investment planning, and tax-saving planning. If you don't have all these, your financial plan is not living up to expectations. It should. It's up to you to make sure that it does.

Don't forget unused contribution room

When I look at unused contribution room, I'm staggered by the number of people who have not made full use of their RRSPs.

Statistics show that only about a third of the country uses RRSPs — though most of the country probably qualifies for them.

There is, in fact, some $180 billion that could have been put in RRSPs but wasn't. Often people don't realize how much they can invest here. One of the reasons is that they are misled by the assessment notices they receive from Revenue Canada after they file their tax returns for the year. Ottawa isn't out to cheat you — this number is based on information you put on your tax return. Perhaps there's additional information you can supply that would increase your contribution limit for the current year.

A couple of things you might consider doing:

If you have a high tax year or if you want to trigger capital gains after a big run-up in the market — and you have unused contribution room — you can always borrow the money and contribute it to your RRSP. If it makes use of this contribution room, hopefully you'll qualify for a whopping tax deduction — and perhaps get back half of the money, which now can be used to pay down the loan.

If, at this stage, you want to trigger a capital gain, it will be taxed at a reduced rate, because only 75% of the gain is taxed. Your RRSP contribution, however, is made at 100% of your marginal rate — with the result you'll end up with a windfall. You can use some of that money to pay off the RRSP loan as well.

Next step: Borrow to buy back your investments or to make other investments. That makes the loan tax deductible, whereas the loan you took out to pay for your RRSP contribution is not. It's all multi-dimensional.

When the question of unused contribution room comes up at seminars — and it always does — I urge individuals not to leave the billions of dollars represented by the tax write-offs in the government's hands. Most people find, in fact, that when they do go back and use up this room, they wish they had done so much earlier. At one point, the government was worried that we would start cashing in on this bonanza. That's why there was a seven-year limit on RRSP carry-forwards. This rule has now been eliminated. But as the pot gets bigger, don't assume that Ottawa won't change the rules again.

If you're not sure how to start, check the assessment notice Revenue Canada sent you. Or call Revenue Canada. It will tell you to the dollar how much you're entitled to put in your RRSP.

That's also something your financial adviser can help you with. It's worth checking out. Good advice for students, too. If you entered the labour force this year, you may have unused RRSP contribution room from the years you were a student. If, for example, you earned $5,000 a year during your summer holidays, it would qualify you for an RRSP contribution, even though it wasn't enough to attract taxation.

How important are guarantees?

Don't be confused when you walk into a financial institution and see that silver CDIC Insurance sign on the door. Don't automatically assume that everything is covered — because it is not.

If guarantees are a concern and you're not satisfied by the returns offered by GICs, you may be interested in finding out a bit more about the Canadian Investor Protection Fund, which is offered by a member of the Investment Dealers' Association firms and a few of the country's largest financial-planning firms. This fund offers $500,000 coverage on deposits. In fact, some of the companies buy extra insurance to take this coverage up to $2.5 million per client.

This is not to cover losses suffered by investors on stocks or mutual funds but solely on investor deposits or cash on hand between transactions. As an investor, you might want to give some thought to doing business with a financial-planning firm or company that offers this level of protection, because when you're waiting for a market correction, you will have much more protection than you would with a bank, a trust company, or a Caisse Populaire. Many credit unions, by the way, offer higher and more flexible coverage than the chartered banks. Considering this and the rates these institutions are currently paying on deposits, not just on savings accounts but on term deposits and GICs, you should be asking yourself if it is really smart to stay with a bank or think about a credit union. Or, for that matter, whether you should have a large amount of money in any deposit-taking institution.

Also keep in mind just what CDIC insurance covers. Essentially, short-term, deposit-type investments like bank accounts, term deposits, and GICs up to $60,000. The insurance has never covered mortgages, mutual funds, or U.S. bank accounts.

There was always some confusion over what was covered. That was partly because, until now, financial institutions were not allowed to talk about the program and what it covered. If you had questions, you were given a brochure or an 800 number to call.

CDIC provides $60,000 worth of insurance per individual. That means you; your RRSP, which is classed as a separate individual; your spouse, who also qualifies as another individual; her RRSP; and a joint account. Grand total — $300,000 worth of coverage at the same institution.

The key question in all this is not whether your money is safe but how much you will get back. And when. Basically, it will be your original investment plus interest.

But guarantees, as we know, come at a price, especially in inflationary times. Inflation may be low now — but don't assume that will always be the case. It won't.

A five-year $10,000 term deposit purchased today — even with an inflation rate of 3% a year — means that your $10,000 will have the purchasing power of only $8,500 in today's dollars.

CDIC insurance gives many people a very important comfort level — but, if not used in a multi-dimensional way, you won't get back what you put in because of inflation.

Bottom line: Guarantees aren't always your best deal.

It's also fair to note that CDIC says it has no immediate plans to lower the $300,000 limit on the stacking of CDIC coverage at one institution.

Be that as it may, we understand that many financial institutions, notably the big banks, would like to see this limit reduced because of the cost of premiums they pay for this coverage. My concern runs somewhat deeper: I have great reservations about having that kind of money on deposit at any institution, not simply because of these fears, but also because it is not really good financial planning. Considering today's interest rate environment and the long-term outlook for interest rates in general, this type of investment will not enable the depositor to reach his or her retirement goals in a meaningful manner.

That's the real cost of CDIC insurance. Ask yourself how much you're losing by running after guarantees. If it's guarantees you want, you can achieve far greater results by diversifying.

Review all your loans

Now that interest rates are at their lowest levels in years, it's a good time to review all your loans — not just your mortgage.

If you took out a consumer loan a couple of years ago that bears a relatively high interest rate, you may find it worthwhile — depending on the terms of the loan — to ask your lender for a better deal.

If your lender won't give you one, another lender probably will. The loan environment is very competitive these days, and lenders are very anxious to place money with good credit risks.

Other lenders will simply pay out your loan — in effect,

transfer it to them — and you'll benefit from either a lower monthly payment or a shorter period in which to pay off the loan. Either way, you're ahead.

If you have a demand loan that has been secured by collateral such as stocks or mutual funds, you may not realize that you may be paying a premium on that loan because the collateral coverage of your loan did not meet your lender's requirements for a preferred rate.

That may have been three or four years ago. Since then, equity markets have risen significantly, and your equity-based mutual funds may not only be worth a lot more today but may also now meet the collateral coverage required by your bank for its best rate. This could also save you a lot of money. A 2% interest rate reduction on a $50,000 loan translates into $1,000 a year in interest savings.

If your mortgage is coming up for renewal, you might want to think about packaging all these loans under your mortgage. I tend to shy away from this approach because I don't like lumping a short-term consumer loan with my mortgage, which is essentially a long-term loan with a long-term amortization schedule. If that loan was taken out to buy investments, and I could tie that loan to a five- or 10-year amortization schedule, I would certainly consider doing so.

Think of it as investment insurance. With a normal demand loan used to buy investments, you might be asked for cash to cover the loan — in the event of a major market sell-off — or, worse still, be required to sell the investment to pay off the loan.

If you have a five-year amortized loan, it doesn't matter what happens in the market today because we know it will be higher five years from now.

By adopting this approach, you'll get not only long-term protection today but also tax relief on the interest on the loan every year for five years plus a lower rate on your consumer loan — a good multi-dimensional strategy.

What about index funds?

Hardly a week goes by that there isn't an article in the *Wall Street Journal* about index funds, which have attracted a lot of interest in recent months in the U.S. Little wonder. In the U.S., most managers do not beat the index, mainly because the U.S. market is more liquid and more efficient.

That's why growing numbers of investors in the U.S. are choosing index funds over managed funds. These investors aren't interested in shooting for the stars or depending on a manager's market savvy — they want to be in funds that provide a decent rate of return.

If you buy an index fund (and many people do without realizing it — in the case of funds that offer foreign exposure while still maintaining full RRSP eligibility), keep in mind that how well it performs depends essentially on how closely it shadows the index. You should also realize that most index funds do not match the indexes they invest in — because of the costs associated in making the investment.

Unwilling to leave well enough alone, some index fund managers try to outperform the index in a number of ways. These include a variety of enhancements, called "tilting." Tilting might include matching the index by sector while doing something different within that sector.

Other enhancements include currency plays or the diversification of the indexes themselves — a broad outlook on European or Asian markets, for example, where you have more than one index.

What do these enhancements add to the process? Perhaps 30 or 50 or 75 basis points.

What they don't do — and can't do — is get that extra 10% you often see with managed funds. It simply doesn't happen.

What investors are beginning to realize is that the performance they get is essentially the result of the inherent performance of the asset class they invest in. In essence, performance is more dependent on asset class than on the fund within that asset class.

If the U.S. market bubbles along at 14% a year, for example, that's likely what most equity funds will earn over time. In the case of EAFE or international markets that produce annual returns of 18% or so, for example, these funds will likely average 16% or 17% a year.

In Canada, where fund managers often beat the market, there is a compelling argument to own funds with good, active management with a solid track record. Here you have to evaluate the effectiveness of managers in areas like stock selection, country weightings, and market timing. When you look at the research done by specialists in the field, it's quite clear that market timing does not work. In the case of stock selection and sector weightings, some managers are better at it than others. The same applies to country weightings.

The trick here is to add attribution analysis to the equation to find out what each manager is not good at. A manager may be a great stock picker but weak on sector or country weightings. Obviously, he or she should concentrate on stock selection.

Another emerging activity is market timing within the market. As a rule, the value side of the market tends to outperform the growth side. At one time, the market favours growth stocks; at another, value stocks. These environments swing back and forth during the course of a market cycle. There is no conclusive evidence that this strategy actually works, either.

Currency risk — how concerned should we be?

The rise of the Japanese yen and the fall of the U.S. dollar a while back focused a lot of attention on currency risk and how it affects our investments.

Whenever you — or a mutual fund — invest directly in another country, you're also investing in that country's currency. And, just like stocks, currencies fluctuate. Sometimes the Canadian dollar, for all kinds of reasons, becomes overpriced in relation to the U.S. dollar and subsequently falls. Sometimes, it becomes underpriced, as we saw early in 1997, and rises.

Much the same scenario is played out in other countries all over the world — the U.S. dollar relative to the Japanese yen or the German mark, or the French franc relative to the Italian lira, and so on. These currencies are fluctuating all the time.

Your risk as an investor comes when you invest outside Canada in a country whose currency falls in relation to our dollar.

Suppose you invested $10,000 in another country's stock market and that investment went up 10% and is now worth $11,000. You'd really be ahead. If, however, the currency of that country dropped by 10%, that $11,000 would now only be worth $10,000 in Canadian funds.

However, whenever there's risk, there's a flip side — opportunity.

The risk is that something can come out of the blue that will bring the value of a country's currency down. If you invest in Japanese stocks, for example, there's a risk the yen could fall in relation to the Canadian dollar. At the same time, there's also the opportunity that the yen will appreciate, in which case it just adds to your return.

If you intend to live in Canada and spend your money in Canada, and the money you invest in Canadian stocks and bonds is to provide you with an income that will be spent in Canada, there is no currency risk.

If, however, you have a portfolio worth $400,000, for example, that's invested in Canada, and you spend half your time living in the U.S., you're at risk. Not that your investment won't be worthwhile. The risk is that the Canadian dollar will go down vis-à-vis the U.S. dollar. If that happens, you won't have enough Canadian dollars to maintain the lifestyle you'd like in the U.S.

Reducing risk

You can reduce this risk by investing some of your money in funds that hold foreign stocks. Besides, foreign markets generally out-perform Canadian markets, and a portion of your money should be in these markets — if only for this reason.

Some mutual funds attempt to reduce currency risk through the use of derivatives and other similar financial instruments. Some do not. They're prepared to accept the risk. And the opportunity.

There is a body of investors who believe that currencies are essentially unforecastable — and if they're unforecastable, there's little point in doing anything; the whole exercise is a mug's game in which there aren't any real winners. So why do it? In a sense, this approach is an abdication of responsibility — but there are many people who subscribe to it.

The problem is that we've not had floating exchange rates long enough to reach any meaningful conclusions about what works and what doesn't, especially since we spent much of this decade in a chaotic, high-inflation, accident-prone environment that produced tremendous shocks within the system.

The stock market and interest rates, on the other hand, have been around for a long time, and a considerable body of knowl-edge and lore has been built up over the years that gives us some signposts along the way.

No real expertise

The same kind of expertise is still a long way off when it comes to the currency markets and how they perform in varying cir-cumstances.

We do have the tools, which, while not perfect, are good gauges. Derivatives are one of these tools. In the early 1990s, they've developed quite a bad reputation, but the fault is not with the tool but with our ability to analyze and make these tools work for us effectively.

The use of derivatives, by the way, is severely restricted by Canadian mutual funds. They can never be used for leveraging or speculative purposes. If your mutual fund uses derivatives to protect its currency positions, ask your financial adviser how successful its hedging strategies have been. If it doesn't use these tools, find out how successful its strategies have been, keeping in mind that there's no clear-cut right or wrong way.

At the end of the day, it's how comfortable you feel.

Lease or buy? It depends on you
— but most of all on the deal

If you're thinking about buying or leasing a car, be sure to do your homework before making up your mind.

Especially if you've been hooked by low advertised monthly leasing payments. Make sure you read the fine print. You'll find that low monthly payments also need a fairly sizeable down payment.

If you want to make larger monthly payments, your down payment can be as low as zero. If you want a low monthly payment, then it's a simple matter of making a larger down payment.

The total — the down payment and the monthly payments over the term of the lease — represents the difference between the guaranteed residual value and the purchase price.

So, should you lease or buy? It depends on the deal and your circumstances. Many people prefer to lease because it doesn't show up as a loan, even though the lease is an equivalent obligation. Many lease simply because it's cheaper.

That equation changes somewhat if you use your car for business. In this instance, you can write off a portion of the interest expense and depreciation — based on the percentage of use for business. If, for example, you use your car 75% of the time for business, you can write off 75% of all expenses.

If you're not in this position, you're better off buying the car for cash and then borrowing against the car to buy mutual funds. This way you make the cost of owning the car — or at least the interest portion of it — tax deductible. That's what I've always done.

It's also a question of what other use you can put the cash to. If I'm buying a car, I'm buying a depreciating asset. That's why it's important to use the car to acquire assets that will go up in value.

As a rule of thumb, if your car isn't a tax deduction, it doesn't make much sense to lease. However, individual circumstances vary. If you're in a position where you don't have much cash and don't want to liquidate a portion of your investment portfolio but need a new car, then it makes a lot of sense to lease.

The question of leasing is part and parcel of the financial-planning process — balancing one alternative against another and coming up with a solution that best meets your needs and circumstances.

Basically, there are two kinds of leases:

* The retail or finance type of lease, offered by most auto manufacturers through their own leasing companies. Under this arrangement, the individual guarantees that the car will have a certain residual value.

* The true or operating type of lease, where the terms are controlled by the number of kilometres driven by the leasee. Most offer the individual an option to purchase at the end of the lease. That figure is determined at the beginning of the lease and is included in the documentation.

Leases come in a variety of terms — usually 24, 36, and 48 months. The best? That, in large measure, will be determined by how much you drive. If you drive more than 40,000 kilometres a year, you should be in no more than a two-year lease. A three-year lease is good for someone who drives between 25,000 and 30,000 kilometres a year. The four-year lease, though not as good in terms of dollars and cents, is better for individuals who drive fewer than 20,000 kilometres a year.

Bond funds — do your homework first

I'm a great exponent of diversification and believe that everyone should include bond funds in his or her portfolio. In selecting a bond fund, I always find it useful to look at two things:

* The risk profile of the fund and whether it's in keeping with my risk tolerance.

* The performance — and management — of the fund.

The biggest thing about investing is knowing what you want. If you walk into a store to buy a suit, you usually don't walk out with a bathing suit. That's because you know what you want. For some strange reason, it's never quite that simple when it comes to investing.

Many investors not only don't do their homework, they often don't really know what they want. Some people will put $300,000 or $400,000 into funds without shopping around. Yet the same people wouldn't dream of buying a $300,000 or $400,000 home without making inquiries.

Above all, you've got to know yourself. Especially how much risk you're prepared to take.

Don't assume that all bond funds are alike or that they're guaranteed like GICs. While the individual bonds in the fund's portfolio are guaranteed, bond funds can be just as volatile as equity funds.

Some bond funds take more risk than others. Make sure you pick one that matches your risk profile. How? Look at past performance. Not at whether the performance was good or bad — we'll get to that later — but how it stacked up against the average returns of the market in general over the same period.

If the average for the market was 10%, for example, where was the fund in relation? Perhaps it posted a 20% return in one year and 0% the next when other funds averaged 8%.

As you track the fund over a period of years — these data are very easy to obtain — you'll know right away if it's a very volatile fund. There's nothing wrong with this as long as that's what you want. If not, stay clear of it, regardless of past performance.

When you assess performance, it's useful to remember that **money managers can never be right all the time. Or wrong all the time.** Also check whether the fund, especially one with a superior track record, is managed by the same people as in the past.

The key is performance. When you're buying a fund, you're buying the management behind it. And if this management has a good track record for the amount of risk you're prepared to tolerate, **the first thing you ensure is that the same manager or investment approach is still in place.** That's important in the case of funds, where outstanding performance can be traced to a certain individual, but certainly not in all cases. Many funds are managed to very specific mandates, and in these cases it is less important.

If you asked me whether I'd buy a baseball team that has a tremendous group of players, I would certainly want to know that these players are still under contract. That's pretty basic.

How long has the individual who manages the fund been around? If the manager of a fund with a super 10-year track record has only been on the job for two years, recognize that you're buying someone else's performance. Above all, look for funds with formulas that win more often than lose — and ensure that these formulas are still there.

One of the big pluses of holding bond funds is that they provide unit-holders with a monthly income. Some investors use this income stream to buy units every month in an equity fund — much as they would in the case of a monthly investment plan, except that the monthly payment is generated by their bond fund.

Using this strategy, their principal is still intact and relatively safe, and if there is a good run in the equity markets, the return on their overall investment will be somewhat bigger than if they just left it in the bond market.

The reinvestment option is one of the great features of mutual funds. In this instance, the income stream isn't used to buy more units in the bond fund but to acquire shares in an entirely different fund. This strategy will also enable you to take advantage of dollar-cost averaging in perhaps more volatile funds than you've been used to.

By buying an emerging-markets fund or a small-cap fund this way, you reduce the downside risk. Dollar-cost averaging is ideal for these types of funds because they average out the cost to investors. If you do decide to buy a bond fund, there are three factors to consider:

* **The quality of the bonds in the fund's portfolio.** No matter how good the yield, if the quality of the bonds in the portfolio is suspect, any gains can be wiped out very quickly. This is especially important in the Canadian corporate bond market, which is relatively thin at the moment. This means that top-quality corporate bonds are more costly and thus do not offer a very attractive yield.

  This doesn't leave much of an option, because you don't want your fund to own poor-quality corporate bonds. Credit quality is critical in a down market. You should be very conscious of this. Some bond and income funds are investing a portion of their assets in royalty trust units. These are high-yield equity investments that are traded on stock exchanges and do not offer the same security as bonds. These are not simple investments, and the tax treatment can vary significantly from one royalty trust unit to another. You have to decide whether you're comfortable with this.

* **The track record of the portfolio manager.** How has the manager weathered past storms in the bond market, and how well did he or she perform in up markets?

* **Your comfort with the way the portfolio has been positioned.** This is important. If you have a strong negative view on interest rates and want to be in short-term bonds, and if the fund you're looking at is in long-term bonds — the completely opposite view — look for one that reflects your view.

Are balanced funds a good substitute? Some are. It really depends on the fund. Some are very restrictive and keep the bond/equity mix of the portfolio in a narrow band.

Ideally, you should choose a fund where the portfolio manager has a lot more leeway to move assets. If we had a massive stock market crash — by 20%, for example — the portfolio manager should be in a position to take full advantage of the situation by going 95% equities. Some balanced funds restrict equity holdings to 60%.

These are extreme circumstances, but they do occur, and your fund should be positioned to take full advantage of a major move in either the equity or the bond market.

The flip side to debt reduction

The flip side to the vigorous cost-cutting programs by various levels of government is a sharp reduction in government debt available to investors. In fact, it's already happening.

This will work to the advantage of bond holders or bond fund investors as the range and quality of government debt either shrink or become relatively static. Whatever the case, top-quality bonds could well be in short supply — and bid up accordingly — if this trend continues. This has already shown up in the supply of top-quality preferreds, long considered an acceptable yield alternative to bonds.

Is there a right time to invest?

This question comes up all the time at seminars — and my answer is always the same. *Yes.* Essentially, it depends on your time horizon. If you're investing for the next six months, timing is everything, but if you're investing for the next 10 or 20 years, it really doesn't matter when you invest — as long as you invest.

Over a 10- or 20-year period, the trend of the stock market is up. Not just a little bit but a lot. That's the way it's been for decades, and there's no reason to presume it will be any different in the next five or 10 years.

Ideally, we would all like to buy when the market is down and sell when it's high. I've never been able to pick the top or bottom of the market — even once — and I don't know anyone else who has with any degree of success, either.

I do know a lot of people, though, who have made, and continue to make, a great deal of money in the market. They did it by buying quality investments, especially mutual funds, and giving their investments time to work.

Time is really the key. At the end of the day, it didn't matter if they bought into the market when stocks were high or low. What mattered was that they were in the market and able to take full advantage of the increase in stock prices when the market turned higher — as it always does after a correction.

It is, of course, the height of irony that when the market

undergoes a correction, investors hesitate on the sidelines when they should be jumping in with both feet. A review of past market sell-offs illustrates what I mean.

In 1957, the stock market sent investors running for cover with a drop of 20.6%. In the next two years, however, it not only recouped this loss but also went on to break new ground, rising 31.3% in 1958 and another 4.6% in 1959 — a total of 35.9% during the two-year period.

In 1962, the stock market posted a 7.1% decline. In 1963, however, it rose by 15.6%, and in 1964 by a whopping 25.4% — a gain of 41% during the two years following a decline. Not a bad trade-off.

There was a virtual rerun in 1966 when the market dropped another 7.1%. What happened in the next two years? A gain of 18.1% in 1967 and another 22.5% in 1968. That's 40.6% against a loss of 7.1%.

In 1969, the market dipped again — by less than 1% — and by 3.6% the following year. What happened in 1971? You guessed it. The market rose 8%, and by another 27.3% in 1972.

Another big sell-off of 25.9% in 1974 was followed by gains of 18.5% in 1975 and 11% in 1976. That's 29.5% for the two-year period.

In 1981, there was a 10.3% drop followed by gains of 5.5% in 1982 and another 35.5% the following year.

Another drop in 1984 — a small one (2.4%) — and again, gains of 25.1% in 1985 and 9% in 1986.

Even 1987 — the year of the big meltdown — posted a small gain, amounting to 5.9% for the year. In 1988 and 1989, there were more gains — 11.1% and 21.4% respectively.

The next major correction came in 1990 when the market dropped 14.8%. In 1991, stocks rebounded with a gain of 12%.

There was another small loss in 1992 (1.4%), followed in 1993 by one of the best years in the history of the market — a gain of 32.6%.

I realize there are a lot of figures here to digest at one time. I offer them to make a point: No matter how much the stock market drops in any given year, it rebounds strongly in the following years.

Almost without exception, the increases that follow a sell-off were significantly higher than any losses that were recorded.

Another yardstick is to look at the number of times stocks posted better returns than either bonds or T-Bills. Here's what happened from 1951 to 1993: On the basis of one year — 20 times out of 43 years; on a five-year basis — 25 times out of 39; on a 10-year basis — 26 times out of 34; and on a 25-year basis — 19 times out of 19.

The conclusion: The longer the time horizon, the more the stock market is apt to outperform other forms of investment.

What about the number of periods stocks posted negative returns? On the basis of one year — 11 times out of 43 years; on a five-year basis — one out of 39; and not once over 10- and 25-year periods.

One final set of numbers to consider. These also concern market timing and show, quite clearly, that **you have to be in the market, good times and bad, to benefit from it.**

One study showed that if you had invested $10,000 in 1956, it would have grown to $298,800 — if left in the market for 30 years. If you had been out of the market during its best six months, your investment would have only grown to $154,100. In comparison, T-Bills would have earned $152,500 during the same period.

Also worth noting: Many mutual funds outperform the TSE Index regularly — providing a cushion on the way down and higher returns on the upside.

So, is there a right time to invest? If you've got a five- or 10- or 15-year time horizon, you can see that it really doesn't matter. If the past is any guide — and it usually is — what matters is being in the market. And staying there.

Foreign markets — great for all the right reasons

Canada accounts for only 3% of the world's capitalization — think of it, just 3% — so why would you bet all your chips on one of the smallest pieces of the pie? This doesn't mean, of course, that 97% of your money should be outside Canada, especially if you have currency or foreign-government concerns, but it does mean you should diversify outside Canada — much the way a mutual fund diversifies its assets among a number of industries rather than focusing on one or two and hoping for the best.

At the moment, there are hints out of Ottawa that the federal government is giving some thought to increasing the 20% foreign content limit for RRSPs. Ironically, one of the reasons has been the success of Ottawa's deficit-cutting program, which has reduced the need for government borrowing. That means that pension funds, mutual funds, and RRSP accounts in general — all big buyers of Canada bonds — will no longer have access to government debt to the same degree in the future. Perhaps Ottawa will open the door a bit to allow RRSPs more foreign exposure, in particular greater exposure to guaranteed foreign government debt.

Aside from hedging ourselves against a weaker Canadian dollar, there are many reasons why we should include a portion of our assets in foreign investments. The biggest is risk and return. Studies show that **global investors have historically enjoyed higher rates of return, and what's more, usually at lower risk.**

International-investment results over the past two decades indicate that it may be more risky, in fact, to limit your investments to just one company or continent. Part of the reason is the narrowness of the Canadian market, which currently represents only about 3% of the world's investment opportunities.

And these opportunities are big — and quite significant.

By limiting ourselves to North America, we would not be able to invest in seven of the 10 largest automobile companies in the world; seven of the 10 largest insurance companies; seven of the 10 largest financial companies; eight of the 10 largest chemical producers; eight of the 10 largest appliance and household-durables manufacturers; eight of the 10 largest electrical and gas utility companies; eight of the 10 top engineering and machinery companies; eight of the 10 biggest electrical/electronics companies; or any of the world's top banking companies or construction and housing companies.

The list goes on, but the point is abundantly clear — we simply cannot afford to ignore the opportunities waiting for us around the world.

If this isn't enough reason, performance should be.

Since 1976, Canada has not once been the best-performing equity market in the world. The U.S., by the way, placed best only once.

The statistics are overpowering:

In 1976, the best-performing market was Hong Kong, which posted a 30.5% gain. In comparison, Canadian markets rose by only 9.2%.

In 1977, it was the U.K., where the market rose by 41.6%. Canadian markets that year rose only 6.2%.

The stats for other years are just as compelling:

1978 — Japan up 54.5% and Canada up 22.3%.

1979 — Hong Kong up 82.8% and Canada up 52.3%.

1980 — Hong Kong again up 73.8% and Canada up 21.6%.

1981 — Singapore/Malaysia up 18% and Canada down 10.1%.

1982 — U.S. up 22.1% and Canada up 2.6%.

1983 — Australia up 55.2% and Canada up 32.4%.

1984 — Hong Kong up 46.9% and Canada down 7.1%.

1985 — Germany up 138.1% and Canada up 16.2%.

1986 — Japan up 101.2% and Canada up 10.8%.

1987 — Japan up 41.0% and Canada up 14.8%.

1988 — Australia up 38.2% and Canada up 17.9%.

1989 — Germany up 48.2% and Canada up 25.2%.

1990 — U.K. up 10.4% and Canada down 12.2%.

1991 — Hong Kong up 49.6% and Canada up 12.1%.

1992 — Hong Kong again up 32.2% and Canada down 11.4%.

Canada, in fact, was at the bottom of the heap — and Hong Kong at the top — in this study.

The top-performing market in 1993 was Turkey, which posted gains of 234% compared with 32.5% for Canada; in 1994, it was Brazil, which rose 76% compared with a loss of 0.32% for Canada; in 1995, Switzerland, which turned in the best performance with a gain of 41% compared with Canada's 14.5%; and, in 1996, Venezuela, which soared 132% while Canadian markets rose 28.3%.

Another point to remember — if you look at the performances of equity markets around the world on a year-by-year basis, it is clear that these markets do not go up or down in unison. There are plenty of examples of markets that produced gains while markets in Canada and elsewhere were in retreat.

The past, of course, is no guarantee of the future. It is a guide, and what it tells me is that a portion of my money has to be in foreign markets.

Some foreign markets are more stable than others and, like Canada, can undergo difficult times as well as good times. Some are very volatile — so pick those markets you feel most comfortable with.

The returns are worth it. In fact, studies show that portfolios utilizing the 20% foreign content earned 1% less than portfolios that maximize foreign holdings.

In the case of a $60,000 investment, that 1% can make quite a difference over 20 or 30 years. A $10,000 investment earning 9% a year will grow to $56,044 in 20 years. A 10% return on the same investment would grow to $67,270 during the same period — or $11,226 more.

Over a 30-year period, the difference is even more striking. That $10,000 earning 9% a year would now be worth $132,676, while a 10% return would grow to $177,494 — a difference of $44,818.

No one can afford to ignore those numbers in investment strategies. Some people, unfortunately, do, especially when it comes to their RRSPS.

They've heard all about the big losses suffered by Asian funds in 1994 and the beating Latin American stocks took in 1995. They simply don't want to take any chances with their retirement money.

Fair enough. Who does? I certainly don't. But there's another side to the equation that often gets overlooked when these markets, especially emerging markets, go into a nosedive: These markets also go up the same way, usually faster and higher — and if you're not in the market at the time, you'll miss part of the ride, usually the best part. In fact, both these markets have not only recovered since then but also produced impressive returns for their unit-holders.

Not all foreign markets behave this way. The U.S. market has consistently set the tone for other world markets for years and is one of the most stable in the world. So are the London and German markets.

These are world-class markets with tremendous liquidity and considerable depth, offering investors a superb opportunity to invest in some of the world's largest corporations.

Aside from returns, foreign markets add another important dimension to portfolios — currency protection. When you invest in U.S. equity funds, for example, the stocks in those funds are U.S. stocks and are denominated in U.S. dollars. This makes a lot of sense most times — and even more during periods of political uncertainty, as we witnessed in Canada during the 1995 referendum in Québec.

The trick is finding the right mix, the right markets, and the right balance. Talk to your financial adviser.

Strategies for a falling market

Biggest mistake investors make in a falling market? Following the day-to-day fluctuations in the market.

People sit around the kitchen table and convince each other they'd be better off out of the market. Or that they should jump in and load up when the market is roaring higher. Their strategies should be exactly the opposite.

They should buy when no one else wants to get into the market. Sooner or later the latter will — and when this happens, the investor with a long-term view will make a killing.

I've used this example before — but it bears repeating: If the local department store has a big sale on — 30% above retail — would you buy? What about a sign that advertised 50% off, one time only? A new car which normally sells for $24,000 that goes on sale for $12,000 would have a lineup of people a mile long to buy it. A 30% drop in the stock market, on the other hand, sends investors running in the opposite direction.

Best approach? Choose investments that enable you to follow a buy-and-hold strategy. That boils down to high-quality blue-chip equity mutual funds or stocks.

By adding a multi-dimensional twist, you can push the enve-lope all the way. It involves selling some of your most profitable investments inside your RRSP to yourself. That's right — to yourself. You can sell any investment inside your RRSP at any time to whomever you wish, including yourself. This will enable you to trigger a tax-free capital gain inside your RRSP and still retain the investment outside your plan. If it holds up, you get a further capital gain; if it drops in value, you'll be able to sell at a capital loss, which will give you a deduction against any capital gains outside your RRSP. Meanwhile, the proceeds of the sale of these investments inside your RRSP can be used to purchase the same investments — at a higher base price — for your RRSP.

In 1981, there was a big sell-off in the market, with many stocks going at real bargain-basement prices. If you had had the courage to jump in then and had held on through all the trials and tribulations of the market since then, you would have walked away with a lot of money. Big money. Those opportunities will come again.

I was at the CBC at the time and can recall the horror stories that came across my desk. Most people were scared. And didn't take advantage of it.

Rates were very, very high — Canada Savings Bonds paid 19.5% that year — and you knew that rates could not be sustained at these levels indefinitely.

At that time, you could have locked in to a long-term Government of Canada Bond at that rate or in an annuity offering the same rate of return. At that time, too, inflation was running around 14% a year. An investor in the 50% tax bracket would actually have had a negative 4% return after taxes and inflation. Today you can get 7% on Government of Canada Bonds, and because we have very little inflation, your after-tax return would be 2%.

You're actually better off today, even though the interest rate is significantly lower.

Performance — if the past is no guarantee, what is?

Past performance, as they say, is no guarantee of future performance.

True. But what is? Ironically, nothing, other than past performance.

When I consider a fund, I take a hard look at three things — its portfolio manager and his or her track record; the makeup of the portfolio; and, above all, the performance of the fund over a three-year, five-year, 10-year, 15-year, or 20-year period. The longer the better. I'm not always impressed by one-month, three-month, or six-month returns, no matter how great they are.

This brings up another point. No manager, no matter how great his or her track record, can be right all the time. Or wrong all the time, either. **Moral: Don't judge a portfolio manager on the basis of six-month or 12-month returns.** It's not that managers lose their touch from time to time. It has more to do with their investment style — and, more specifically, whether their investment style is in sync with the market.

There are four basic equity-investment management styles, and each is in favour at a different time in the market:

* **Price-driven managers** who look for stocks that are undervalued.

* **Earnings-growth managers** who select stocks on the basis of earnings.

* **Market-oriented managers** who invest on the basis of sectors.

* **Small-cap managers** who seek out emerging companies with potential.

Some managers change their style in an attempt to keep in vogue. Unfortunately, this strategy doesn't always work.

Here are some other considerations:

* Whose past performance are you buying? If the fund manager has moved on, will the fund still produce the same level of returns? Research suggests that funds tend to fade after a management change.

* Growing assets may force a change in style. A small-cap fund,

for example, may be forced to change its focus and consider mid-cap or big-cap stocks once a certain asset base is reached.

* Some periods reward different management styles. If you're a value manager, that is, you invest in stocks with perceived value and hold them until they realize their potential, your fund will obviously do better than in a speculative environment, which tends to favour small-cap managers.

* Some periods favour certain sectors within the same asset class. In periods when there is an inverted yield curve, T-Bills and mortgages, for example, may outperform bond funds.

Above all, remember, mutual funds are not a short-term investment.

Don't rely on any one asset class

The retreat into certainty and security — essentially into GICs and term deposits — is a timely reminder about the dangers of relying on one asset class to meet your financial goals.

As a rule of thumb, you'll always do better if you diversify, if you include all asset classes — bonds, stocks, GICs, etc. — in your portfolio. Many people have a difficult time coming to grips with this because they aren't knowledgeable about investing — with the result that many become savers rather than investors.

A lot of people who bought mutual funds last year were basically savers who weren't happy with the rate they were being offered on GICs at the time and switched over to mutual funds. Essentially, for the wrong reasons. They had expectations that weren't fulfilled, so they retreated back to GICs in disappointment. They would have been far better off to have kept some of their money in GICs or term deposits, and some in bond or equity funds to take advantage of any upturn in these markets.

As a general rule — and this applies to all investment classes, including GICS — your investments will not realize their full potential by relying on one class. **Sooner or later, you will lose out.**

If you put all your money into the stock market, you're happy if it goes up and unhappy if it goes down. If all your money is in real estate, you're unhappy if you can't sell it when you want.

Always diversify. That, in essence, is one of the values of a bond mutual fund — as opposed to a bond, or a zero coupon bond or a strip coupon bond. With a bond mutual fund, the portfolio manager can diversify around the world — so if the Canadian dollar comes under pressure, your investment will still do reasonably well, because some of your money will be invested in bonds from Germany, Britain, France, the U.S., etc.

Bond funds solve another problem — what term to buy. Interest rates are in a straight line or on a flat yield curve at the moment.

What should I do? Buy long-term bonds? If I do, will short-term rates rise faster? If I buy short-term bonds, will long-term bonds rise more?

With a bond fund, you have someone who follows this market around the world, every day, to make that decision and the kind of mix of terms and countries that will provide the best returns.

Next thing: Make sure there is a mix.

That's another reason why you should select an independent financial planner — she will break down the mix and, based on her judgement, select one bond fund that meets your criteria over another.

Diversification is also why mutual funds have done so well over the years.

What's a realistic rate of return?

Don't get too comfortable with those big double-digit returns produced by high-flying equity funds in recent years. They won't last. I'm talking not about a downturn that is waiting to happen — and will happen — but about the kind of returns we can reasonably expect the market to produce over the next 10 years.

According to the Toronto Stock Exchange, the rate is 10% to 11% a year. That's the average compounded rate of return recorded by the TSE over the past 25 to 40 years — and a realistic benchmark to shoot for. These are good returns that are achievable without a great deal of grief along the way. Let me illustrate: At 10% a year, your money will double every 7.2 years; at 11%, every 6.5 years.

All of which underline the importance of staying invested and, above all, sticking to an investment strategy that works for you and your portfolio. That includes not running lickety-split after the latest hot fund that may or may not produce the kind of returns you'll expect down the road.

Creating tomorrow's portfolio

If you had a chance to create an entirely new portfolio, what would you put in it? If it is different from your current portfolio, then seriously consider changing what you have.

Just go back 12 months and see how you would have allocated your portfolio — asset class by asset class. What percentage would you put in equities or equity funds? How much in bond funds? What percentage would you keep in cash? This is what makes asset allocation so interesting and why some investors do better than others.

When you deal in assets, you're always balancing today's prices against any changes in tomorrow's expectations. What's important is not how that asset — a stock or a bond — performed today or yesterday, but what it will do next year and the year after that. And, above all, how your choices reflect your long-term goals.

You have to stick with a strategy and not be diverted by the circumstances of the moment — unless you think what is happening represents a fundamental shift of the economy that will affect the long-term risk and return of the various asset classes within your portfolio.

In developing this strategy, decide what you're saving for. Define your risk/return objectives — the amount of risk you're prepared to take to reach your financial goals. Determine your needs, especially your need for liquidity, your investment time horizon, and tax considerations.

Chapter 4

Lifestyle Strategies

*Where does a doctor in Florida
send his patients to recuperate?*

Finding money for your nest egg

I'm constantly asked by people how they can get enough money together to begin an investment program. Without money, they add, all the advice I offer them is virtually useless.

The reason these individuals don't have money in the first place is that they usually don't have a plan. That's critical — because if you don't have a plan, you're not going anywhere, no matter what you're trying to achieve. Most football teams go into every game with a specific plan. It's the only hope they have of winning. Each side has a plan and a strategy as to how it will play the game, offensively as well as defensively. Usually, it's the team with the best plan that wins over the long term. Not just the team whose plan will work that particular day, but the team whose plan will get them to the Superbowl.

You have to think the same way. The reason why many people come up short is that they're paying too much tax. That's where you should start, too.

First step is to sit down and do a budget. Find out where your money is going — especially how much is taken by the tax collector. In fact, if you ask people what their biggest expenditure is, they'll probably tell you it's their mortgage. They're always surprised to find it's their tax bill.

And that, ironically, is where you'll find the money to get the ball rolling:

* **Take every tax deduction you can get.** People believe they don't have any money left over to put into an RRSP, but often the same people may be sitting on $5,000 worth of Canada Savings Bonds. If you're in this position, put the bonds in your RRSP. The government will give you $2,500 or so in tax savings — just for doing this. Now you've got the money to start your investment program.

* **Defer taxes wherever possible.** Learn how you can legally pay these taxes later — without incurring any interest costs or penalties — because if you can defer payment, you'll have use of that money to make investments until you do have to pay it back. Even if it's only $1,000, that $1,000 will sooner or later double — but your tax bill won't. It will stay the same.

* **Invest the money you save through tax deferrals** at the highest rate you can get without incurring a lot of risk. You don't want to lose this money, because you'll have to pay it back at some point. What you want is an investment that will grow at a reasonable rate of return — so that you'll be able to pay it back at any time and keep the money earned on this investment.

Here's what I mean: Suppose I am able to save $5,000 by

deferring taxes. If I could double that money in five years, it would grow to $10,000. If I paid back the $5,000, I'd have $5,000 left for investing. If I held on to that money for another five years, I'd have $20,000. Five years more — a total of 15 years — it would turn into $40,000. If I kept it for another five years, that investment would be worth $80,000 — thanks to the magic of compounding and, above all, time.

By using this strategy, you've not only frozen your tax bill, but you're also able to keep all the growth that money generated over a five- or 10- or 15-year period. That's why tax deferral is such a superb deal for investors.

* **Invest in assets, not debt.** No one will ever get ahead by simply earning interest income. Revenue Canada will give you all kinds of tax write-offs if you buy investments that have the potential of earning it future profits. If you buy something that is absolutely guaranteed — a term deposit or GIC — you pay the full tax. There are no tax write-offs. Remember, too, interest rates are largely a reflection of inflation. As a rule, if inflation goes up, so will interest rates.

This brings us to another point worth noting — when you subtract inflation and taxes from the interest paid on GICs and other guaranteed investments, you'll find that there's very little left over.

GICs and term deposits are great places for your money if you're concerned about safety or if you want to park it somewhere while you're waiting to take a position — but in the long term, the only place you'll get the kind of returns you want is in income-producing assets — mutual funds, stocks, and rental real estate. And in that order.

Historically, these assets appreciate in value. Everybody, however, has a pain threshold. That pain is fear. So your comfort level will determine what mix of investments you should have in your portfolio.

The GIC Trap

A lot of investors cash out of mutual funds during a market sell-off and move back into GICs — usually at precisely the wrong time.

A good move? Not in my books. GICs are old investment technology, and investors should weigh the pros and cons of locking away their money for the next three or four years.

Many investment professionals share these views, including Gordon Garmaise, president of Garmaise Investment Technologies, the architect of Mackenzie Financial's Star Program.

First of all, says Garmaise, while GICs in modest quantities can have an appropriate role in a portfolio, they are not as risk-free as many investors think. "If you bought a five-year GIC that yielded 5% and found that you could get 9% on the same type of GIC the following year, you might not feel that the investment you made a year ago was riskless," explains Garmaise. "In effect, you're losing out on the return you could have had if you had bought a one-year GIC and then reinvested the proceeds in a five-year term this year."

BETTING ON INTEREST RATES

When you buy an individual GIC, Garmaise adds, you're betting that interest rates will not rise during the term of the investment. If rates rise during this period, you would be better off with a money market fund. This would give you the flexibility to acquire a five-year GIC after rates have risen.

If, however, rates fell during the period, you would have been better off putting your money into a bond fund — because bond funds rise in value when interest rates fall.

Also, and this is a point Garmaise stresses, GICs have not provided as good a rate of return as a mutual fund portfolio over the long term. In 1977, the year he formed Garmaise Investment

Technologies, had you invested $1 in a typical portfolio of GICs, it would have grown to $7.17 at the end of 1996 — an average annual rate of return of 10.6%.

GICS VS. MUTUAL FUNDS

In comparison, that $1 invested in a balanced portfolio of assets — 40% in Canadian equities; 40% in bonds; 12% in U.S. equities; and 8% in international equities — would have risen to $11.48. That's 60% more, or an average annual return of 13.3%.

Shorter periods of return told the same story: Over one year, a mutual fund portfolio would have outperformed GICs 66% of the time; over a five-year period, 75% of the time; and over 10-year periods, 97% of the time.

The lesson: If you buy mutual funds, even after rates have gone up, you'll do dramatically better than buying GICs at what is considered the optimal time to buy GICs.

INTERNATIONAL EXPOSURE

GICs don't offer international currency protection — a key point today. That, too, is one of the advantages of mutual funds, which can offer international currency and underlying market diversification — protection you just can't get with GICs.

Final point: Term deposits and GICs offer little protection to investors in terms of inflation.

In 1977, if you invested $100,000 and withdrew $9,000 a year — indexed to the rate of inflation — you would have had to withdraw $9,512 the same year just to keep up with inflation.

Today, you would need to take out almost $25,000 a year just to give you the same purchasing power you had in 1977. Not so easy if you had put that $100,000 in a savings account. Your money would have run out in 1987. You would not have earned enough interest to offset inflation — and would have been forced to dip into your capital very early on.

If you put those funds in a short-term money market, your money would have run out in 1990.

In a good-quality mutual fund, however, that money would have provided regular payments totalling $364,283 over this period. But with one big difference — your investment would now be worth $658,083.

There is also a tax consideration. Income produced by GICs or term deposits is taxable at full marginal rates. Withdrawals from mutual funds, on the other hand, attract a lower tax liability.

Think of your investments as a balloon on a string. When you buy an investment that offers a guaranteed return — like a GIC or a term deposit — you're just getting the string. The balloon is the capital gain. If you want the balloon and the string — the interest and the capital gain — then invest in a bond or a bond mutual fund. You'll get the same rate of return, the same guarantees, but you'll also get a capital gain when rates fall.

Stocks or real estate?

The correct answer is *yes*. If you own a house — and you should, because a home helps you establish roots — you can borrow against it and use the proceeds to invest. Now you've got growth as well as roots.

Your house may rise or fall in value, but regardless of what happens to real estate prices, it gives you a place to live and a place in the community. But it's your investments that are going to make you money over the long term.

In terms of pure investment, it's the stock market every time. In fact, real estate doesn't even come close — even though it should help you keep pace with inflation.

This, of course, doesn't mean that you should sell your home and use the proceeds to buy mutual funds. Using your house as an asset, however, to raise money for investments could prove very valuable and enable you to get the best of both worlds. That's why you should think of your home as one of the basics — unless circumstances dictate otherwise.

Two studies — one by Dynamic and another by Trimark — make it very, very clear that when it comes to investing, the stock market is the place to be. Nothing else comes close.

The Dynamic study tracked the return on a $70,830 home in Toronto at the end of 1979. This was the average price of a home sold through the Toronto Real Estate Board at that time. The study compares the return on this home with the return on a five-year GIC and the rate of inflation, and notes what the same investment would have earned by Dynamic's Income Fund.

That $70,830 home was worth $215,638 in 1997 — a gain of 204.4% over the 20-year period. Inflation during this period amounted to 121.5%, growing at an annual compound rate of 4.79%. In dollar terms, that amounts to $156,911 just to stay even.

A similar investment in five-year GICs would have produced much higher returns. Here your original $70,830 investment in 1979 would have grown to $358,812. That represents a gain of 406% or an annual compound rate of return of 10.01% over the same period.

The same money invested in Dynamic's Income Fund at the end of 1979 would have grown to $465,400 by the end of December 1996 — a 557% return, representing an annual compound rate of return of 11.71% over the period.

The Trimark study is just as compelling. It tracks the return on real estate in 12 Canadian cities over a 15-year period — from September 30, 1981, to March 31, 1997. A home in the greater Vancouver area in 1981, for example, sold at $199,000. In 1997, it was valued at $304,354. The same amount invested in Trimark Fund would have risen to $2,604,910, and to $1,556,770 in the case of Trimark's Canadian Fund.

The difference is even more striking in the case of real estate in the Prairies.

A home in Calgary, valued at $300,000 in 1981, would have risen to $338,000 in 1997. A similar investment in Trimark Fund would have been worth $3,927,000.

In Edmonton, a $229,000 home actually dropped in value to $210,000 in 1997. The same investment in Trimark Fund would have been worth $2,997,610.

A home in Regina, worth $126,500 in 1981, would now be worth $132,500. This compares with $1,655,885 if that money had been invested in Trimark.

In Toronto, a $225,000 home in 1981 was selling for $495,000 in 1997. That money in Trimark would have risen in value to $2,945,250.

A similar picture emerges in Mississauga and Ottawa. In Mississauga, a $129,000 home would now be worth $193,365, and a $120,000 home in Ottawa would have risen in value to $200,000. Similar investments in Trimark Fund would have yielded $1,688,610 and $1,570,800 respectively.

A similar picture emerged in Montreal, where a home valued at $220,000 in 1981 would now be worth $380,000. The same investment in Trimark Fund would have been worth $2,879,800.

This is a lot to digest at one sitting, but the message is quite clear — **the stock market outperforms virtually any other kind of investment over a 10- or 15-year period** and underscores the reason why at least a part of your investment funds must be in equities or equity funds.

Segregated funds —
if you want guarantees . . .

If you'd like to invest in equity funds but are more comfortable with fixed-income investments like GICs, you might want to take a look at segregated funds.

Segregated funds are sold by life insurance companies (although Mackenzie has a special balanced fund that will also guarantee your original investment). As the name implies, the assets of segregated funds must be kept and managed separate from the general assets of the life insurance company.

Like mutual funds, segregated funds invest in a wide range of fixed-income and equity securities and can be bought and sold at any time at current values. Unlike mutual funds, segregated funds contain a guarantee that not less than 75% of your money — in some cases, 100% — will be returned at the end of the contract, usually 10 years, or on your death. These funds are also creditor-proof — if the designated beneficiary is the fund-holder's spouse, child, or grandchild.

Another advantage — probate fees can be avoided. And many of these funds offer excellent returns over a 10-year period.

There are also some disadvantages — liquidity is usually restricted; many segregated funds require monthly premiums (unlike the Mackenzie fund); sales commissions can sometimes be high; and investment information is not readily available. Also, you don't have the option of taking out your dividends. These must be reinvested.

The 10-year return on these funds, as I noted earlier, has been quite strong. But then again, so was the 10-year return on a wide range of well-known mutual funds. In fact, you would not have lost a penny by investing in any of these funds — even among the poorest performers — over the 10-year period.

So how much is this guarantee really worth? It's great to have, of course, if that's what you need to be able to sleep at night, but you lose a lot of flexibility in the process. And you will certainly miss out on some of the best-performing funds and, above all, the ability to tap into some of the best investment minds in the world.

Remember, guarantees come at a price. Remember, too, rapid changes are taking place in the world today. Make sure you're positioned to take full advantage of them.

What matters in the end, of course, are your investment objectives, the level of your risk tolerance, and whether you are comfortable with your investments.

Income-splitting strategies

All income-splitting strategies start with one basic premise — the more you earn, the higher the percentage you pay to the government. In the U.S., you can file a joint tax return — and at least get some relief through income splitting — but in Canada, married or not, each of us has to file a return and get dinged accordingly.

In essence, one spouse can be earning a ton of dough and another earning very little. The higher-income spouse pays a higher penalty per dollar of income than the lower-income spouse. That's why it's critical to move as much of our income as possible to the lower-income spouse's name or to the names of our children.

In addition to straight income tax savings, there are other values that may have a bearing on the Canada Pension Plan and RRSP contribution limits, etc.

If, for example, a husband earns more than his wife, she should keep all of the investment earnings for the family in her name. In this instance, the wife, who has a smaller salary, or no salary at all, would be taxed at a lower rate. If the investment income is lopped off the husband's income, which is taxed at a much higher rate, the family gets to keep a larger amount.

If you have concerns about the family splitting up — that's a marital problem, by the way, not a financial one — you should understand that in most provinces now the estate would be split evenly between spouses.

Let's look at a few ways to split income that may be appropriate for your situation:

Pay your spouse a salary. All you need is a business that is operating — it doesn't need to be incorporated to do this — and you can put your spouse or, for that matter, your children on the payroll and pay them an income equal to what you would normally pay someone else to do the same job. In this instance, the salary you pay your spouse qualifies as a tax deduction from your income or your company's income, and your spouse earns that income at a lower rate and even qualifies for an RRSP based on that income — so that he or she would wind up paying very little tax in the final analysis.

Ditto for your children. Keep in mind that children — or anyone else, for that matter — can earn about $6,500 before their income becomes taxable. If you pay your child $6,500, you'll be able to claim a $6,500 tax deduction, and your child will earn that money tax-free. That's a double advantage and a good example of multi-dimensional thinking.

Income split using a non-incorporated business to save money on your tax return. Here's what I mean: Suppose you have a landscaping business that you operate from your home on a part-time basis. Because it's a business, you can write off part of your garage and some of the equipment you use in the business. In this scenario, the business is not incorporated, and it is near the break-even level. If you were to pay your spouse out of the business, which would cause it to lose money, the bottom five lines of page one of your federal tax return would show negative income. That negative income is deductible against your other income — including your salary, interest, dividends, and capital gains earned.

This is another classic multi-dimensional strategy: You wind up with a tax deduction against the income from your full-time job, your spouse ends up with income that is taxed but at a much lower rate, and your children earn income that isn't taxed at all.

Lend money to your spouse. In the old days, you could just give a pool of money to your spouse and he or she would pay tax on the income produced by this money. Not so today. What you can do, however — and this is a point many people miss — is lend money to your lower-income spouse.

Suppose you lend $100,000 to your husband, who is in a lower tax bracket than you, and he invests this money, which earns 10% or $10,000 a year. Current attribution rules require you to pay tax on this $10,000, but not — and this is a key point — on the income it earns. That income is taxed in your husband's hands.

However, if you have a legitimate loan on which you charge the going rate of interest, then what really happens is that you pay tax on the interest he pays you on the $100,000 loan. The rate charged is usually the prescribed rate set by the government. Like other rates, it also fluctuates from time to time.

Let's say you lend this money to your husband at 5%. You would receive $5,000 in interest income that is taxable at your marginal rate. If you had invested the $100,000 in your name instead — and it also earned $10,000 — you would pay tax on this income at your higher rate. Now, if your husband invests this money, which earns the same $10,000, here's what happens: He would be taxed on this $10,000 — but at his lower rate. In addition, he gets a $5,000 deduction on the interest he pays to you. Bottom line: The family benefits from having $5,000 of this income which is taxed at a lower rate.

Now, if your husband earns even more on the investment, the story gets better. If his investment is able to return 12% or 13% a year — many mutual funds do over a five- or seven-year period — you still only pay tax on the $5,000, again at your rate, but your husband will pay tax on any excess, which could be as much as 8%, 9%, or even 10%. This means even greater savings for the family.

The objective of this exercise is to get as much money, earning the highest rate possible, in the name of the lower-income spouse and, at the same time, to keep as little investment income as possible going to the higher-income spouse.

You can also benefit by giving your spouse money — provided your spouse does not invest the money. Suppose, for example, you earn $50,000 and your wife $20,000 and you give her enough money to pay her income tax. By using this strategy, she is able to keep the money she would have paid in taxes and can now invest this money in her own name, without attribution to you.

The same principle applies if you give your child $50,000 to buy a home. There's no attribution because this money does not produce an income. Or if you give your wife $5,000 to contribute to her RRSP. Here, too, your wife is not investing the money. It's her RRSP, which is considered another individual by Revenue Canada, that's investing these funds. By using this strategy, you effectively lower the pool of money available to produce taxable income. Instead, your wife now has $5,000 inside her RRSP — again, without attribution to you. In fact, your wife gets a tax rebate, which can now be invested in her name and any earnings taxed at her lower rate as well.

Where there are two working spouses, it pays to have the lower-income spouse keep as much of his money to invest as possible. The higher-income spouse should pay all the family's operating bills until she has exhausted her pool of money. What you're trying to do is get the lower-income spouse to build as much money as possible in his name because it will be taxed at a lower rate, while the higher-income spouse spends the bulk of her money.

Spending is one thing. Investing quite another. While maximizing RRSP contributions should top the list of every tax strategy, **the higher-income spouse might give some thought to putting the maximum, not in his or her RRSP,** but in a spousal RRSP. Here the higher-income spouse gets the big tax deduction and the lower-income spouse gets the money. This will produce a bigger income for your spouse on retirement than he or she would normally have.

Best of all, you're also putting in place a long-term income-splitting strategy that also includes CPP, your investment income, your principal residence, and your RRSP.

When it comes to spousal RRSPs, you have to look forward a bit as well. At the moment, you may have a husband who earns more than you. You, however, may stand to inherit a lot of money down the road or may be planning to enter the workforce in the near future in a profession where your earnings potential and pension would be substantially greater than your husband's.

Or you may be sitting on non-income-producing assets such as a real estate portfolio which you know you will eventually liquidate. When this does occur, you will have a larger pool of money to invest than your husband. In these situations, it's only logical that you should not be doing as much income splitting as you might do otherwise — because you'll only be loading up with income that will be taxed in a disadvantaged manner when you retire.

Without question, the federal and provincial governments are doing a bang-up job of paying down their deficits. This means that eventually governments will bow to pressure and lower income tax rates — all the more reason why we should be taking every tax deduction we can today.

That's especially important in the case of income splitting. As a rule of thumb, the higher earner should take as big a tax deduction as possible now, so that any income produced in the lower earner's name will be taxed at an even lower rate when tax rates are eventually reduced. Historically, governments tend to lower tax rates for lower-income earners faster than for upper-income earners.

In the case of income splitting with children, there are several things you should consider: If you give money to a child who is under age 18 and who earns income on this money either through interest or dividend-paying investments, you — and not the child — must pay tax on this income under current attribution rules.

This is not as valuable as if the child invests into something that produces a capital gain, because there is no attribution in the case of capital gains. That means we should all try to put whatever we can in our children's names, ideally into long-term capital gains-producing investments.

Once the child is 18 or over, you can give him as much as you want for him to invest in any way he wants — without any attribution whatsoever.

However, if you have an 18-year-old living at home — or even someone older — think about giving him money to invest which will enable him to produce an income which will be taxed at his rate. An important point, because he can earn $6,500 or so and pay no tax at all.

By adopting this strategy, your family will be saving tax on $6,500, which will now be available to pay some of your household expenses like education. Effectively, you'll wind up with tax-free income.

If your child is 18 or over and you give her money to contribute to her RRSP, there is no attribution, either. She also gets a tax deduction on her contribution and can give you the tax rebate. In the meantime, the money inside your RRSP will compound tax-free.

If the child is still receiving the Child Tax Benefit, another set of rules comes into play. First, this benefit is tax-free money. It's meant for the child's use. If she chooses to invest it — hopefully, with your guidance — there is no attribution on the income produced by this investment, either. In fact, the investment will grow tax-free in her name — so that you should always try to give her at least the amount of the Child Tax Benefit.

Attribution does occur, however, if you give money to your child and she puts it in dividend-paying mutual funds, for example, or in interest-bearing investments. The first level of income will be taxed in your hands. Secondary income — income earned on the first level of income — will be taxed in the child's name. That's because you've already paid tax on the first year's income. Each first year's income from then on will always be attributed to you. You should segregate this income and show that the second and third levels of income generated on the initial income are taxed in the child's name — and at her lower rate.

Income splitting is even more critical for seniors as it becomes more important to keep incomes below the clawback line. Here are a few suggestions that may work for you as you enter retirement:

* **Consider splitting Canada Pension Plan payments** — a valuable strategy if your spouse receives a lower amount. Apply to Health and Welfare Canada.

* **If you're nearing retirement — and your projected RRSP income, plus Old Age Security and Canada Pension Plan, are nearing the clawback level — think of maximizing spousal RRSP contributions rather than your own.** This is especially important if your spouse has been out of the workforce for some time, has reduced CPP benefits, and is far from the OAS clawback level. This strategy will enable you to receive full OAS benefits and higher RRSP income during your retirement, and your spouse to qualify for a higher income stream from his or her RRSP than would otherwise be the case.

Suppose you just won the lottery

If your lottery numbers come up, before you do anything, get some tax advice — especially if you want to share some of your luck. If you do, you have to make sure you don't have to pay tax on any earnings this money may produce should the person you're giving it to decide to invest it.

This is called attribution — a rule introduced by Revenue Canada to reduce income splitting between family members.

Once you fully understand the tax consequences of any action you might undertake, put the money in a 30-day T-Bill or in a money market fund. And then blow town.

Don't quit your job or change anything for the time being. Just blow town for a month. Ask for vacation time or, if need be, a leave of absence, but do get out of town.

Even then, you'll be surprised how popular you've become. You'll hear from people you haven't heard from in years, every relative, even people who wish they were relatives. In fact, there will be people who are prepared to change their names to become your relative. You'll also find that salespeople are wonderfully intuitive in tracking down lottery winners. They'll be seeking you out to give you a lot of great ideas about how you should invest your money.

When you disappear for 30 days, keep in mind that the vacation will be virtually free. The earnings of your lottery winnings — especially if it's a big one — will more than offset any loss in income you might suffer by being off work for a month.

During this period, talk to your financial adviser. Ask him or her to do an analysis of your financial situation in light of your newfound wealth. Should you pay off your mortgage? What about your debts? Basically, all the things you should do before investing a cent of the money.

The answer in most cases would be *yes*, especially if your debts are not tax deductible.

Where do you invest this money? And should you give some of it away? Rather than giving it away outright, you may want to put the money in a trust — so the beneficiary will get an assured income during the life of the trust.

We all hear about people who get a windfall and yet become destitute a few years later. With a trust, you can make sure the beneficiaries, perhaps your children or your spouse, will be looked after — in spite of themselves — now and in the future.

I mentioned earlier the importance of not quitting your job. One reason is life insurance. It may not seem all that important to you at the moment, but it may be very important a year or so from now — should you suddenly find yourself with a major health problem.

By quitting your job, you may be giving up a group plan that could be converted into a paid-up policy. Also, you may be giving up disability and other benefits — even a pool of pension money. If you don't leave your job on good terms, that money may come to you minus the company's share.

With $2 or $3 million in your hip pocket, these things may not seem all that critical, but they could be vastly important to you, your family, and your overall asset pool down the road.

Perhaps you or one of your children would like to use this money to start a business. If so, you might be better off just tucking your money away for a year or even taking an educational course while you're still employed. This way you'll have the time to seek out a business you want to invest in while you're still learning. The last thing you want to do is just quit your job and move on. Or invest your money unwisely. And once the word is out that you've won the lottery, you'll have all kinds of hare-brained schemes come your way.

Best approach: Take your money and put it in a pool of assets in which you have some flexibility. That applies whether you're buying mutual funds or a stock portfolio. Flexibility is important, if only to ensure that there's always money in the pool to buy a car or some other major item.

You don't need to invest it all. Keep in mind that a couple of million dollars will earn enough — even in a money market fund — to buy a car in a few days. So why spend the principal when, in fact, you can take the earnings and buy the car?

Inheritances

In most cases, inherited money arrives tax-free. From then on, though, Revenue Canada will tax any investment income earned once the money is invested. That's why it pays to receive any inheritances in the right person's name.

For example, when a family inherits money, it pays to split it evenly between spouses where possible. That way, one-half of the yield will be taxed in the lower-income spouse's name, if, in fact, it is taxable at all.

In addition, choosing investments that produce dividends, capital gains, or rental income can allow us to earn substantially more before we are taxable. The dividend tax credit, in fact, allows us to earn as much as $22,000 in tax-free dividends from Canadian corporations; we pay tax on only three-quarters of any capital gains; and rental income can be offset by any expenses associated with operating a building and, when profitable, capital cost allowances.

The other consideration, of course, is long-term. If one spouse is going to have a much better pension than the other, this type of tax planning can pay off in future years. Arranging to have future income mature in the name of the spouse who has a small or no pension will mean that this income will be taxed at a lower rate.

Don't forget when your spouse qualifies for Old Age Security that he or she will automatically be lost as a tax deduction.

It's important to take the time to sit down with a financial adviser, accountant, or tax lawyer before you receive or utilize any inheritance. It may even be possible to put some of the money into your children's names so it can earn even more investment income tax-free.

Forced savings plans work — if you don't have one, create one

You'd be surprised — I know I always am — by the number of people who use their income tax deductions as a forced savings plan. In most cases, I realize, it's because we don't want to be caught short with a big bill at tax time. Even here, you'd be much further ahead stashing that money away every month in a savings account that would at least earn you interest until tax time rolls in again.

The reason people have a hard time doing this, I find, is because they are finely attuned to the consequences of not having this money at tax time. It's an incentive we all understand.

We can, however, create our own forced savings programs — and our own incentives — to build a pretty big nest egg that will enable us to live better today and most certainly in retirement.

The reason tax deductions work is that, for most salaried people, what they don't see they don't miss. You can do the same thing yourself — arrange to have $100, $200, or even $500 deducted from your pay every month and put into an investment.

You can do that now with Canada Savings Bonds on the payroll savings plan or invest in credit union shares where you work. Some companies encourage their employees to buy company stock through monthly deductions.

Most mutual fund companies offer the same facility through monthly savings plans. These programs enable you to save as little as $50 a month, which will automatically be deducted from your bank account.

All you need is incentive — and a goal to shoot for.

One of the big sports stories of 1997 was Davis Love III's dramatic win of the PGA Championship in August. Behind that win was a story and a personal loss. His father, a golf pro, had died in a plane crash in 1988. The tragedy affected Davis deeply, but he kept on golfing, winning one tournament here and another there — but never hitting it big until the PGA. The picture that made the papers the next day showed a rainbow over the green where he putted in a pouring rain. The rain didn't stop Davis. Nor did personal tragedy. He kept on playing throughout it all, and when it was time to reach for the gold ring, it was his.

There's a pot of gold at the end of the rainbow for each of us, providing we stay the course, too. That's why a systematic savings program is so critical to helping us meet our financial goals — today and tomorrow. It's just another way of paying ourselves first. And it works.

Your mortgage is a prime example. It's a form of forced savings plan — with a big carrot. If you stop making monthly payments, you lose your house. But you can create your own forced savings plan — and the incentive to make sure it works, too.

If you put that money in a savings account, you might earn enough to buy a colour TV or take a vacation. With Canada Savings Bonds, you earn a higher rate of return, but not enough to do anything meaningful. What about mutual funds? They will give you a much higher long-term growth — if you stick with them. Or should the forced savings plan be in your RRSP, where you can get tax relief on the contribution? Great multi-dimensional thinking can add new zip to any savings program.

Joint investments

As I travel the country, I'm regularly asked how families should handle investments that are purchased jointly.

The classic example involves sharing income earned in a joint account. Can it be split in any way that would be advantageous to the couple? It would be nice if it could. Then we'd all claim the interest earned in these accounts in the lower-income spouse's name.

Revenue Canada, however, is wise to that plan. It wants us to claim the interest earned in joint accounts — and any other jointly held investments, for that matter — based on the amount of money each partner contributed. Technically, you should compare your income with that of your spouse and prorate the interest earned on that basis. If only one spouse works, it's hard to believe that the other spouse could have earned any of the income generated by the joint account. However, if your spouse brought some money into the family from a previous job or an inheritance, it could be argued that some of the interest earned in the joint account is taxable in his or her name.

When one spouse has no income, you must be careful when moving income to that spouse's name. While he or she can earn more than $6,100 income before becoming taxable, once the spouse earns more than $525, the dependent tax credit will be eroded.

If both spouses work, you would normally prorate the interest earned on the difference between salaries. However, with a little financial planning, it may be possible to have the lower-income spouse claim as much interest income as possible. The tax burden will be lower.

Let's say the husband is the higher-taxed spouse. The family should try to use his income first. That way the family can justify leaving the wife's earnings in the joint account longer — and they can show that the wife keeps and invests the bulk of her salary while the husband spends all or most of his.

As a result, you should be able to argue that the bulk of interest earned in a joint account belongs to, and should be taxed at, the lower-income spouse's rate.

Similar strategies can work with other investments. If you buy term deposits, try to justify them in the lower-income spouse's name. If you buy stocks and mutual funds, though, you should do an extra calculation first. It involves dividends from Canadian corporations which qualify for the dividend tax credit. This credit can only be used when you have tax to pay. This means you should assess how much income your spouse will earn in a year. If he or she is not taxable, it's better for the higher-income spouse to earn the dividends.

It's not unusual for spouses to buy rental real estate properties jointly. When you do, you should be careful. If both spouses do not contribute to the project, Revenue Canada will want all taxes recorded in the higher-income spouse's name. If there are tax deductions involved, the tax relief generated would be better in the hands of the higher-income spouse.

In the case of profits, however, you should try to justify some of the earnings in the lower-income spouse's name. If each spouse contributes the same amount to the purchase and maintenance of the building, you should have no problem justifying joint ownership. If each spouse does not contribute cash, it's still possible to justify some joint sharing. If one spouse contributes the cash, the other should handle all the work — the cleaning, management, renting, etc. — as a way of justifying joint ownership.

A written marriage contract
avoids problems later

If you or one of your children plans to get married soon, put some thought into the financial aspects of the union. I believe everyone should go into marriage with a written contract.

This may seem like an inappropriate time to discuss splitting up, but statistics show that marriages which have a written contract tend to survive better than those that don't.

Under the Family Law Act, you must split everything in half in the event of a breakup. In that unhappy event, there will be no need to decide who gets what because that will have already been decided in the marriage contract.

This contract should also deal with child support, in particular how much money will be needed if you are living alone, taking into consideration the tax implications of this support.

Usually, the husband pays money to the wife, and, according

to a recent landmark court ruling, the wife gets this money tax-free.

Whatever the situation, figure out how much the care-giving spouse should get after taxes. If it is $500 a month, your lawyer should mark this amount up to $700. The spouse who pays the $700 will get a tax deduction. Also factor in what the payment should be if the support payments are conWrmed as tax-free or the payments are no longer deductible for the spouse making them.

Every agreement should be written in stone.

Living together was always more beneficial — in terms of taxes — than getting married. I say "was" because the rules have been changed. Couples who live together for one full year are now considered married in the eyes of Revenue Canada. (If you and your common-law partner have a child and live together, you're instantly married under the tax law, whether you've lived together for a full year or not.)

They no longer enjoy beneficial income-splitting strategies. That includes owning two tax-free houses. So now there's no real advantage to living together — at least as far as income taxes are concerned. If you take advantage of income-splitting rules — being able to move money from one spouse to another — it's more beneficial now to be married.

Turn summer camp into a tax deduction

For some families, one of the great joys about summer is being able to pack the kids off to camp. It's good for them and even better for you. The only fly in the ointment is the cost — and that can be quite hefty. There is, however, a way to ease the pain by getting Revenue Canada to pick up part of the tab. It revolves around Revenue Canada's definition of day-care.

When I look back at summer camp, what comes to mind is a

group of guys or gals sitting around the campfire or enjoying water sports all day. Fortunately, Revenue Canada doesn't share my memory. It's far more liberal. To Revenue Canada, any camp can qualify as day-care. That includes computer camp or hockey or baseball camp — any camp, in fact, that you, as a parent, use for day-care purposes.

Here's how the rules work:

If you're married and pay for day-care, only the lower-income spouse can claim child-care expenses. The deduction is limited to $5,000 for each child under age seven and $3,000 for children seven to 15 years of age. For children age six or under on December 31 of the year claimed, you can deduct up to $5,000 per child — with no maximum for the family.

When it comes to summer or day camp, however, a different set of numbers comes into play — up to a maximum of $150 a week for each child under the age of seven and $120 a week for children age seven to 14. If the child is disabled and over 14, you can also claim $120 a week.

Key point to remember — only the lower-income spouse can claim, and only if both spouses work. The deduction is intended not to help us pay for baby-sitters but to help us go to work and earn income that we share with the tax collector.

There is also a way to claim day-care expenses when neither spouse works. If the wife, for example, is enrolled in an occupational training course for which she gets an occupational training allowance under the National Training Act, or if she carries on research for which she gets a grant, day-care can be claimed.

There's also one other seldom-used exception: If one spouse is confined to jail for at least two weeks, the other spouse can claim day-care as though he or she were a single parent.

Single parents are able to claim for child-care expenses regardless of income — unless the children live with the other parent. In this situation, married rules apply, and only the lower-income spouse is able to claim the deduction.

Married couples in which only one spouse works are not allowed to claim child-care expenses at all.

Day-care fees are normally paid to a registered institution or an individual who provides personal day-care services. We can pay a relative as long as this relative is at least 18 years old. A minor can also qualify — providing he or she is not a relative.

If you're self-employed, there's another strategy you can use that also includes Revenue Canada as your partner in sharing the costs of summer camp. Self-employed individuals can hire their own children for various jobs — but not (and this is critical) at a higher wage than you would pay a nonrelative.

If you pay your child throughout the year, you'll get a tax deduction at your high rate, while your child — or anyone, for that matter — is able to earn $6,000 a year tax-free.

Bottom line: Your child will now have the money to pay for summer camp, and you'll have a tax deduction, which may, in fact, be higher than what you might ordinarily claim under day-care rules — great multi-dimensional thinking.

Another strategy is to invest the child-benefit cheques in your child's name. By doing this, the income produced by the investment is taxed in the child's name, not yours. That means zero in most cases. Over time, your child will be able to pay for his own summer camp with tax-free income — at substantial savings to you.

You can also give your child a sum of money he can invest as his own. Under current tax rules, any income produced by this investment must be taxed in your name. However, any investment income produced by this initial income is taxed in your child's hands. Over time, this can also add up to a substantial amount every year which will also likely be tax-free.

If you want Revenue Canada to share in the costs of sending your son or daughter to summer camp, do a bit of planning. Your child will benefit — and so will you at tax time.

What about time shares?

If you're thinking about buying a time share, think twice. Even three times, if necessary.

I know some people who swear by them. One of my friends has a ski lodge and, under his time-share agreement, gets to go there two weeks every year — the two weeks he wants — and over the years he's built up friendships with the people who go there at the same time. That's something he might not be able to do if he rented. And that's what he wants.

Too many time-share properties are vastly overpriced, however. Think about it. If you pay $10,000 for the right to occupy a unit for one week, it means the unit really costs $500,000 — and that's allowing two weeks for maintenance during the year. It should be one sweet condo at that price — but very, very few of them unfortunately are.

Other negatives: You have no control over how well the building, or even your unit, is managed or maintained, or over the people — the other owners — with whom you're sharing the unit.

Better choice — buy a condo unit and rent it out to others when you're not using it. This way other people will help to pay for the unit, you'll have some say over how the building is managed and maintained and about the type of individuals you want to rent it to, and, best of all, you'll get first crack every year on the weeks you want to occupy the unit.

There are negatives with ownership, too, of course. You're the landlord in every sense of the word, with all the responsibilities and costs that ownership entails. In contrast, time shares are very simple and offer another advantage — the opportunity to trade your unit with the owner of another time-share unit somewhere else. There are no guarantees, of course, and you pay an extra fee for this.

There's a new slant that's caught my attention — it puts a new spin on time shares that may be worth considering. One of the big negatives about time shares is that most people tire of going to the same place year after year — with the result that many time-share owners put their two weeks into a pool or try to swap them for another two weeks at some other time share, perhaps in a more exotic location.

A new twist has been added to make these arrangements more flexible. You get points which you can accumulate. If you don't use them this year, you can add them to the points you'll earn the next year and get an absolutely stunning condo over the Mediterranean. Think of them as frequent-flyer points that give you more options and more places to choose from.

Pool or cottage?

From an investment point of view, a cottage wins over a pool every time. It's more expensive to buy, the upkeep is more costly, but a cottage does pay off in the long term.

A pool is cheaper to install, much, much less costly to maintain, but it can diminish the value of your property. Many people don't realize this, but it does — mainly because a pool narrows down the number of people who might buy your property should you wish to sell, especially in a down market.

The rationale is very simple. There's a sizeable number of individuals who don't want a home with a pool — older people who often prefer a garden in their backyards, young parents concerned about the safety of their children. In a slow market, having a pool can actually make your home harder to sell. I know some people have a hard time believing this — because they think a pool adds value to their home — but it's true.

Even so, there is a big trend today of people building their cottage at home. They're putting in hot tubs, pools, saunas, everything they can, because their home — as principal residence — is the only thing left that's tax-free.

On the plus side, the use of a pool is much greater because there's no driving time. It's right there in your backyard.

At the same time, maintenance of a cottage can be a killer. And very time-consuming. You have to drive up to it and spend hours every spring opening it up for the summer and even more hours closing it for the fall. Then there's insurance, utilities, maintenance, not to mention a second set of furniture.

A cottage, however, can be used year-round if it's located in the right area, while a pool can only really be used during the summer months. Also, a cottage will rise in value, especially if it's located on a lakefront.

A cottage may not be your best answer

Summer is getting into high gear, sales of cottages are surging on a wide front, and prices are firming — and even rising in many areas. If you've been holding off, do a little soul-searching before taking the final plunge.

Anytime I hear of a surge of activity in any investment, the first thing I ask myself is: *Why is everyone selling?*

Usually, it's for a number of reasons — perhaps for tax considerations or lifestyle changes, a death in the family, or even a change in jobs.

What about the buyers? Many include investors whose pockets are jingling with money from a big score in the stock market. In other cases, it's individuals whose lifestyles have changed, and they are now in a position to afford a second property. For still others, it's a chance to speculate on the old sayings about cottages, including one I've heard all my life — they aren't making waterfront property anymore.

Whatever the reason, most people don't spend enough time thinking about the total picture before they buy a second property.

First, there's the cost of money. If you borrow to buy a cottage that you intend to use most or all the time yourself, keep in mind that the interest on any loans or mortgages is not tax deductible. The best way around this is to sell some of your investments and use the cash to buy the cottage. Then borrow to buy back the same investments. This simple strategy will make your interest cost tax deductible.

If you made a killing in the market and have the cash to put up, you will have to think about capital gains taxes and the level of commissions on your stock transactions.

Cottages don't come cheap. You know the purchase price — but there's also maintenance, insurance, utilities, and all the other expenses that come with owning a second property to pay on an ongoing basis. These are not tax deductible — unless you're renting out the property. In that case, they can be claimed against the rental income. Keep in mind, however, that these expenses can only be deducted if there's reasonable expectation of a profit and future appreciation. Using your cottage part-time and renting it out part-time seldom cuts it with Revenue Canada.

And while you're at it, give some thought to how much time you'll actually be using the property. To get a good purchase price, you'll have to do some driving. Three hours on a Friday and three more hours on a Sunday night may not be your idea of fun, especially if you only get to use the cottage during the summer months. Year-round use could make it more attractive, of course.

Then there are taxes. Under current tax rules, we can claim the capital gains exemption only on our principal residences. If you rent in the heart of the business district, for example, you can buy a cottage and claim it as your principal residence — even though you don't live there full-time. This way it will rise in value tax-free.

When you factor in the costs of maintenance, taxes, transportation (time and actual cost), cottages represent a major expense affordable by only a few.

Bottom line: You'll probably do better — in terms of lifestyle and capital gains — by adding amenities to your principal residence.

Check on investments
coming up for renewal

It's important to review your investments, especially those that are coming up for renewal, particularly GICs that may be part of your RRSP. These are automatically reinvested for another term — unless you instruct your bank or trust company otherwise. You have to be very careful about this, particularly if you've made up your mind you don't want to invest in GICs again.

You have to do something about it. What usually happens is that you receive a notice from the bank or trust company where you have GIC investments, informing you that your GICs are coming due. If you ignore the notices — and many people do — your money is automatically reinvested, in many cases, at the lowest rate available.

You should be assessing every dollar you have in RRSPs and deciding what you're going to do with each investment. You should ask yourself if you're happy with today's interest rates. Are there alternatives? What about mortgage-backed securities — if absolute guarantees are important? Should some of your money be in the European market? Or in other types of investments like stocks or mutual funds? The point of this assessment is to decide whether you want even a portion of your investments automatically renewed.

Moving: Expenses are tax deductible if . . .

If you moved to a different city this year — or are planning to do so sometime in the near future — there's a good chance Ottawa will pay part of your moving expenses.

There is an "if," of course. To qualify, your move must be in conjunction with a job change. In the case of a job-related move, your residence must be at least 40 kilometres closer to your new place of employment.

Many people think that if they move 40 kilometres or more, they automatically qualify for this deduction. **Not so. You must change jobs.** And your new residence must be at least 40 kilometres closer to your new job.

If you're transferred from one city to another by your employer — and the company picks up the tab — then the company will get a full tax deduction for this expenditure.

Also, you do not have to include on your tax return the money received from your employer for this purpose. In many cases, however, the employer picks up part of the cost, leaving the individual to bear the rest. Your share, of course, is deductible.

What items are considered tax deductible? Just about everything — the packing, transporting, and unpacking. That includes van rentals, even the chicken and beer if you're doing the job yourself, and any other legitimate expense.

If you travel to another city, you may incur travel costs — air and bus fare, gas, oil, meals, even hotel bills while your furniture is being packed or is on the way to your new home, or even while you're waiting for your belongings to arrive. All expenses incurred by your immediate family, including pets, will normally be accepted.

Also, if you own a house, you can include land-transfer taxes, real estate costs, and sales taxes if you buy another property.

All in all, these expenditures can represent quite a deduction.

You will not, however, be allowed to claim the cost of any improvements made to your existing home to make it more saleable. The reason — capital gains on your principal residence are tax-free. Any costs, Revenue Canada reasons, incurred to increase its value — and earn additional tax-free profit — are capital expenditures and are not allowed as an expense.

There is an overlap in some cases. If your employer pays part of your expenses, be sure to claim the balance as an expense deduction on your return. And if you move later in the year, don't worry if your expenses are greater than the income earned from your new job after the move. Any excess moving expenses may be claimed against income earned in the following year.

One other point to consider, and it's a crucial one. Revenue Canada taxes you according to the province where you live on December 31 of each year. So, if you move to Calgary on December 31, you would be taxed at the normal federal rate, but the provincial rate would be lower than in Ontario. That's really the key to this exercise. Basically, you should try — if you have the option — to move to a province where you will be taxed at the lowest possible rate on the final day of the year.

If, for example, you're being transferred to Alberta from Quebec or Newfoundland, where provincial rates are substantially higher, you'll get a whopping tax rebate because of all the taxes deducted from your pay at higher rates throughout the year while you were living in these other provinces.

It also works in reverse. If you live in Alberta and receive a transfer late in the year to Ontario, where the provincial tax rate is higher, you'll wind up with a big tax hit because you would not have had enough tax deducted at source during much of the year.

We know most moves are made during the summer. The second-biggest time is near the end of the year. That's something you can also take advantage of if you're a small-business owner and selling your business, and planning to move anyway — you can effectively pay for your move simply by going to Alberta, where there is no sales tax, a lower capital gains tax, and a lower provincial tax rate.

Home insurance

If you want to get the best deal possible on homeowner's insurance, the first step is to shop around. The second is to deal with a medium to large brokerage.

The reason is that larger brokerages usually have access to a lot more insurance companies than a smaller office does — and are able to shop the market on your behalf, much the same way a large, independent financial-planning firm does for life insurance and other financial products such as tax shelters for its clients.

The third step is to make sure that you're insuring your home for **Full Replacement Value.** "If you do, and your home is under 35 years old, most insurance companies will cover you for **Guaranteed Replacement Cost** — meaning, in the event of a total loss, they will pay the full replacement value, regardless of the limit on your policy," says Brian Olsen, a veteran insurance broker and a principal of Olsen-Sottile Insurance Brokers Inc. in Niagara Falls.

Many insurance companies, he notes, also allow credits that can reduce your premiums even more. These include:

* Age of dwelling — if built less than 10 years ago.

* Claims-free discount.

* Alarm system.

* Age of insured — some seniors' discounts start at age 35.

* Nonsmoker.

* Neighbourhood Watch.

* Sprinkler system.

* Car and home insurance with the same insurance company.

Taken together, it's possible to cut basic premiums by as much as 45% — so talk to your broker to determine if you're eligible for any of these credits.

Increasing basic deductibles can add further savings. Most homeowner policies today have either a $200 or $300 deductible. Increasing it to $500 or even $1,000 will create additional savings.

"Sometimes, if you have an older home that hasn't been updated, you may be in a higher rating classification. If all the facilities have been updated," Olsen notes, "you could qualify for a lower-rated policy." Each case is different, but these suggestions are an excellent starting point in any discussion with your insurance broker to ensure that you get the best possible coverage at the best possible price.

"Remember," Olsen adds, "you pay for what you get. Sometimes the cheapest price is not the best — especially when you suffer a loss."

Note: Automatic withdrawal is also available for all standard market policies in Ontario. The extra cost — 3% a year.

Your home is a great forced savings plan —
so is your RRSP

Young people often ask whether they should use their savings to buy a home or acquire investments or contribute to their RRSPs.

My answer is always the same: You're better off contributing to your RRSP because you'll get a tax deduction — and then using the money inside your RRSP, plus other savings you may have, as a down payment for a home.

Aside from the fact that real estate prices are very low at the moment, a home gives you not only a roof over your head but also a place in the community and — best of all — a forced savings plan. Once you start on a systematic savings plan — whether as payments to your mortgage or to a mutual fund monthly purchase plan or whatever, you're going to do well down the road. The real winners are those who consistently put away money.

The beauty of owning a home is that you have an asset that historically holds its value over a reasonable period of time — recent experiences notwithstanding.

That's why financial institutions are regularly prepared to lend you money against it.

If you borrow a reasonable amount on your home — an amount you can afford to service — you can use these funds to buy mutual funds, in effect, on a monthly basis, because that's how you'll be paying back the loan. The only difference is that the interest on the loan is tax deductible. Now you have a multi-dimensional investment, which is the only way most people win.

Buy your new car in advance

At some point, most of us will have to bite the bullet and replace our cars. Some people solve the problem by opting for leasing and replacing their cars every two or three years. Unless you put a lot of mileage on your car every year or are in a position to write off a big chunk of the monthly payment, this may not be the way to go — especially if you plan to keep the new car for seven, eight, or even 10 years, as many owners are now doing.

With a little financial planning, you can take a lot of the sting out of the transaction.

Let's assume you plan to buy a new car four years from now that costs $24,000. If you take out a four-year loan for this amount at an interest rate of 10% a year, interest costs on that loan will amount to $4,980. This will bring the total cost of your new car (interest and principal) to $28,980.

Why not reverse the process? Instead of making monthly payments after you get the car, why not make monthly payments in advance to a mutual fund that averages 10% a year? Many dividend funds, for example, will do this over a four-year period. So will some blue-chip equity funds.

To accumulate $24,000 over 48 months at 10% a year, you would have to make a monthly payment of $409.10 — or a total of $19,636.80 over the four-year period.

The difference between making monthly payments before and after buying a $24,000 car — $9,263.20. And for most of us, that's in after-tax dollars.

You can save a bit more by putting up $2,500 at the outset. This will lower your monthly payments to $346.71 and your total outlay over the four-year period to $19,142.08 ($2,500 plus $16,642.08 in monthly payments). The difference between buying your car in advance and paying for it after you buy it now grows to $9,757.92.

These are big numbers that demonstrate very clearly what a little bit of advance planning can do for your pocketbook.

What if your bank makes a mistake?

Banks do, of course, make mistakes. Sometimes in the bank's favour. Sometimes in yours. It can be as simple as transferring money into the wrong account, causing you to incur unnecessary service charges or bounced cheques.

The bank will go out of its way to correct the mistakes — if you catch them. That's why it pays to review your statements carefully when they come in every month.

You'd be surprised at the daisy-chain effect. If you're away at year-end, for example, when there are a lot of nonbanking days, you might not clear your Amex or Visa bill, which, in turn, would trigger your cell-phone bill if you use your card to pay your telephone bills. This could also mean that you may be without cellular services. But you won't know until it happens.

If there's a shortfall in your account, will it reflect on automatic transactions such as monthly-purchase RRSP contributions, mortgage payments, and other automatic computer-processed transactions? And who picks up the tab for all these related service charges? Usually, the bank will waive them — if you can show that it has been at fault.

What should you do if the mistake is in your favour? Should you call the bank and let it know or wait and see if it finds the error and contacts you?

If you've just completed a number of transactions and are genuinely not sure, I would recommend that you go back to the bank and explain you think there's been an error. Ask the bank to backtrack and make sure everything is correct. If the bank is reluctant to do this, explain that you fear there is a mistake in your favour. I doubt if the bank would be anxious to give you a fat reward — even if the amount of money involved is substantial — but it will certainly view you as a valued customer and will probably be open to future mortgage negotiations or breaks in service charges.

This may be a good time to mention bank charges and service fees. In a low-interest rate environment, we have a tendency to concentrate on getting a higher yield on our savings and a lower cost on our loans. We should also be looking closely at service fees. A savings account that pays next to nothing could, in fact, be costing you money when all the service fees are factored in.

Year-end checklist

We all have clunkers in our portfolios — a stock that went down after we bought it and shows no signs of reviving in the immediate future. Year-end is the time to get rid of these investments — and get a tax-free capital gain in the bargain.

The reason is that capital losses can only be used to offset capital gains. If you have a capital loss but no capital gains to offset the loss, it can be carried forward indefinitely against future capital gains or carried as far back as three years to offset past capital gains. Either way, it's an effective tax strategy.

There is a caveat, however. You cannot buy the investment back within 30 days for a tax-loss sale to become effective. But there are things you can do. If you sell a nonperforming bond fund on which you've lost money, for example, you can lock in the loss by selling it and buying another bond fund immediately from another mutual fund company.

The net result is the same — you still have a bond fund, but here you also have a capital loss to apply against a capital gain.

Other actions you must take before the end of the year:

If you turned 69 this year, your RRSP must be converted to a RRIF or an annuity by December 31. If you don't convert it, Revenue Canada takes the view that you've cashed in your RRSP, and the entire amount will be taxed accordingly. You have, however, the option of basing your RRIF conversion on either your age or your spouse's, whichever is lower. To maximize your retirement income, you're better off allowing your RRSP to compound tax-free for as long as possible.

Your tax rate is based on the province in which you're living on New Year's Eve. If you move from a high-tax province, like Newfoundland, to a low-tax province, like Alberta, it can make quite a difference in your final tax bill. It also works the other way.

Bottom line: If you're planning to move to another province in the near future, do it when it makes the most sense.

A couple of other points worth noting at year-end:

* If you use a company car and your personal use is less than 50%, be sure to notify your employer by December 31 if you

want the cost benefit based on half the standby charge. If you don't, you'll have to pay 13 cents for every kilometre of personal use, less any reimbursements.

* Make deductible payments such as child-care and alimony before the end of the year. New rules went into effect, and deductions now apply only to agreements signed after April 30. Alimony is not affected.

Chapter 5

Mortgage Magic

*Money isn't everything. But when you're
buying real estate, it can mean a lot.*

Getting a better deal on your mortgage

Do you automatically renew your mortgage at the rate offered by
your lender? Or do you ask for a better deal? Many people are
not only asking for — and getting — a better rate but also taking
it one step further and playing one lender off against the other.

If you aren't, you should be. The lending industry is more
competitive than ever before, and there's never been a better time
to negotiate to the fullest.

What can you negotiate? Just about everything — the rate, the
term, the amount, the prepayment privileges, the penalties, even
the branch you deal with. And you should. You should go in
knowing that. Too many people think they're at the mercy of

their lender and have to accept the offer given to them. Generally, that's not the case. In my experience, there's always something you can ask for to better your position. In fact, more than you imagined.

Let's look at the rate first. The mortgage market is not expanding the way it did in the 1970s and 1980s, and the competition between lenders for your business is intense, to say the least. They know it's a lot cheaper to hang on to existing customers than to attract new ones. For starters, they charge you a renewal fee in most cases anyway — so it's almost no-cost business for them. To attract a new client, they have to incur time, labour, appraisals, legals, and other related costs.

Considering today's market, the least you should ask for is a discount of one-half of one percent off the quoted rate. You might not get that much — or you may, depending on your lender's needs at the time — but you will get something: a quarter of one percent reduction or the elimination of the renewal fee. Everything helps. Especially if you keep your monthly payment at the level paid under your old rate. By adopting this strategy, the excess will be paid directly against the principal of your loan.

Perhaps you'll be offered a lower rate by the competition. It almost always pays to let the competition know you have a loan with another lender. This tells them you've been approved by someone else. An inexpensive credit search will be faster and easier than a full credit assessment of you and your property. And for most banks, taking business away from one of their competitors is always attractive.

But don't wait until the last minute. As your renewal date approaches, you should be talking to as many as a half-dozen other lenders. Remember that banks, trust companies, credit unions, and life insurance companies compete with each other for this business. Also, their rates can vary from day to day.

If an institution has a group of mortgages that have just been paid off, it will be far more hungry for your business because it is flush with cash and wants to get it invested as soon as possible. Conversely, if it has just granted a whack of loans, it may not be in the market at all.

If shopping the market is not your cup of tea, you might want to consider using a mortgage broker. Some charge a fee for their services, but the savings may be far greater than any such cost. Most brokers have a stable of lenders who compete with each other to fund their needs. These lenders pay finders' fees for your business — so that you don't need to. This type of mortgage broker can be very valuable in helping you shop for the best deal at little or no cost.

Most borrowers I talk to don't bother to negotiate. They think they're lucky enough just to get the loan. The lenders, however, want your business — so make them work for it. Also remember, you can always negotiate better prepayment terms. As a rule, most lenders will allow you to pay an extra 10% a year against the outstanding principal of your mortgage. You never know when you might run into some extra cash, so negotiating for a 20% yearly privilege in advance might pay off handsomely one day. Or what about asking your lender for the right to accumulate any unused prepayment limits? In five or 10 years, you could have a completely open mortgage with a lower rate that is usually offered on closed mortgages.

You may also be able to negotiate the elimination of discharge fees and penalties. Even if you are not able to, you should be aware of one fee-saving strategy. If you're discharging your mortgage to move somewhere else, ask the new lender to offset the fees and your old lender to apply the 10% or 20% prepayment to the outstanding balance before any fees or penalties are applied. You'll save a chunk.

I know it sounds strange to think you can negotiate with your lenders — despite the impression they may leave you with — but you can always let them know you're shopping the market. It almost always works.

How to make your mortgage tax deductible

You can make your mortgage tax deductible, and not just your mortgage but every loan you make. It's an important multi-dimensional approach that can make a significant difference in your actual after-tax cost.

How big of a difference? If you're in a 50% tax bracket, that 7% mortgage you've just negotiated will actually cost you about 14% in pre-tax dollars. If the interest is tax deductible, the interest cost in pre-tax dollars would be 7% but only 3.5% in after-tax dollars. On a $100,000 mortgage, that's an enormous saving. In the first instance, it means you've got to earn $14,000 in pre-tax dollars just to pay the $7,000 in interest on your mortgage. This compares with $3,500 in after-tax dollars if the interest is tax deductible.

As with most things, though, you have to do your homework to make sure you don't make mistakes. A wrong decision, especially in the case of your mortgage, could prove very, very costly.

Here's what I mean: Consider the person who owns a principal residence that has no mortgage on it. She borrows against this property to buy a second property which she intends to rent. Normally, the interest she pays on this mortgage is tax deductible. Now consider the case of another individual who owns a duplex. He borrows against the paid-up value of the duplex to buy a new single-family principal residence for him and his family. His claim for interest as a tax deduction will be denied — even though he used the investment property as collateral to borrow the money.

The two transactions look very similar, but in Revenue Canada's eyes, only one is acceptable. To make interest tax deductible, several criteria must be met. First, money must be borrowed, and it must be used for investment purposes. Second, it must be invested in an asset that produces a regular rate of return plus the expectation of a future profit. The absence of either of these criteria can eliminate the interest on the loan as a tax deduction.

In the first instance, the interest should be tax deductible because the money borrowed was used to buy rental real estate, an asset that produces a regular income, and one that historically rises in value over time. You will note that I say "should" in referring to the deductibility of interest, because there will be years when repairs, maintenance, insurance, etc. may well exceed rental income. Normally, you're allowed to carry the excess expenses against other forms of income, such as salary or investment income. If these expenses wipe out all your income, you can still carry them back to previous years or even forward to save on future taxes.

It may be worth noting that Revenue Canada has been carefully monitoring rental real estate investments, and in some cases taxpayers are being denied their real estate deductions simply because there does not appear to be any expectation of profit. If, for example, the real estate was part of a limited partnership purchased at the height of the real estate frenzy in the late 1980s, Revenue Canada might take the view that the value has fallen so far that it cannot see the property ever making a profit. All the more reason to buy real estate that is fairly priced before the tax consequences of the investment are considered.

One question that often arises during my seminars is how long Revenue Canada will allow a landlord to declare negative income on a rental property. There is no set answer. As a rule of thumb, it seems to be acceptable as long as it appears there are *reasonable expectations* of future profit. In fact, many owners buy unprofitable multiple rental properties by borrowing against properties with a positive cash flow. Here one property pays for the other, to produce an overall positive return and tax relief. It would be hard to argue that this practice, while not generating tax revenues, would not produce a potential future profit.

In the second example, the tax deductions would clearly be denied if discovered in an audit, simply because the money was borrowed not to buy a profit-making investment or to invest in a business but to buy a principal residence. The point to keep in mind here — and it applies to loans for other activities as well — is that it isn't the collateral used that determines tax deductibility. It's the end use of the money.

What can be done in this situation? The best strategy would be to sell the investment property, use the cash to buy the new principal residence outright, and then use the property to borrow to make a new investment. In this instance, the interest will be tax deductible because it is clearly an investment loan.

When real estate is involved, this could be an expensive process. This strategy does work wonderfully, however, with other investments such as mutual funds and stocks. They are easier and less costly to sell and buy than real estate. Be careful here, though, because Revenue Canada frowns upon selling an investment and then buying it right back. You should hold it for at least 30 days or, better still, consider buying a similar but different investment.

Your mortgage or your RRSP?

The answer again is *yes*. You put the money into your RRSP and use the tax rebate to pay down your mortgage. It's simple mathematics. Just ask yourself: *What is my mortgage rate, and what is my tax rate?* When you look at it this way, it's quite clear that you'll save much more on taxes than paying down your mortgage.

If your mortgage rate is 7%, for example, and you pay down your mortgage by $10,000, your interest savings every year thereafter will be $700. If you put the same money inside your RRSP instead, all you have to do is earn over 7% and you'll earn more money tax-free than you'll save paying down your mortgage.

Next, take the tax rebate, which will amount to about $5,000, and pay it against your mortgage. That will save you $350 a year in interest.

Here's what you'll end up with using this strategy — $10,000 inside your RRSP, which earns about $1,000; a $5,000 pay-down of your mortgage; and a $350 annual saving in interest costs. Compare this with just lopping $10,000 off your mortgage and saving $700 a year in interest.

The success of this strategy hinges on using your RRSP tax rebate to pay down your mortgage. It's also worth noting that a good-quality mutual fund should provide a compounded rate of return of 10% or more a year — so your gains would be even greater.

Always, always think in multi-dimensional terms — especially when it comes to your mortgage. Suppose you have $25,000. Take the first $10,000 and invest it inside your RRSP and use the balance to pay down your mortgage — the rationale being that your mortgage is a non-tax-deductible expense. You'll save not only interest expense but also tax dollars you have to earn to pay this expense. This is important because, if your mortgage rate is 7%, you could be paying as much as 14% in pre-tax dollars.

At the same time, I like investments, too. Take the $15,000 left over after investing in your RRSP and put it against your mortgage, as in the example. Then turn around and borrow the same amount — by adding to your mortgage or taking out a personal loan, it doesn't matter — and use this money for investment purposes. This makes the interest on that loan tax deductible.

What you've really done is kept the same amount of debt — but made $15,000 of it tax deductible. This simple move effectively lowers the interest cost of your loan to 3.5% in after-tax dollars.

This approach also works if you have a number of deposits — term deposits, GICs, or Canada Savings Bonds — coming up for renewal. Take that money and, rather than reinvesting it, put it all against your mortgage; then, again using the same strategy, borrow an equal amount and reinvest the proceeds. Net result: You'll save taxes and still have an investment. Mind you, I wouldn't borrow to buy back term deposits or GICs, but I would in the case of stocks and mutual funds, or even rental real estate.

If you have stocks, bonds, and mutual funds outside your RRSP, think about triggering capital gains. Don't just automatically sell these investments and take a capital gain and then turn around and borrow to buy the investments back. Do some number-crunching first. The capital gains tax may have a bearing on whether it's the right move for you. Go through the exercise with your financial planner to determine whether, in fact, it is the right strategy.

Depending on your loan, it may not be worthwhile paying down your mortgage. Suppose you're able to pay $200 extra against your mortgage. However, if you're an aggressive person — and not everyone is — you might borrow $20,000 and use the money to buy even more investments. You can service this loan easily — that is, pay interest only — with the $200 instead. If you invest the $20,000 in a high-quality blue-chip equity fund, the interest on the loan is tax deductible, again because it is being used for investment purposes.

Suppose I applied that $200 extra a month to my mortgage instead. I'd save $168 a year for the life of the mortgage, whereas the $2,400 a year I'd pay in interest charges on the loan will net me a tax deduction for the same amount which will save me at least $1,000 a year in taxes. That's a much better trade-off in my books.

As the $20,000 investment grows — let's say it doubles over the next seven years (many mutual funds do) — that investment will enable you to put down an extra $12,500 in after-tax money on your mortgage. That, by the way, also includes paying off your loan.

In the meantime, you'll also be able to take the $1,000 tax rebate you received as a result of the interest deduction on your loan and apply it against your mortgage as well. Using this strategy, you'll be able to reduce your mortgage by $19,500 at the end of seven years ($7,000 in tax rebates and $12,500 in after-tax capital gains). This represents an interest saving of $1,365 every year on your mortgage thereafter.

Do you know how much your mortgage is costing you?

Most people don't know what their mortgage really costs. They confuse the posted or nominal rate — the rate banks and companies advertise — with the effective rate. This is the rate most people pay, and it is always higher.

This is because most mortgages — about 95% in Canada — are compounded semiannually. Therefore, a 7.15% mortgage amortized over 25 years is actually 7.27%. The difference doesn't appear to be much, but it can represent hundreds of dollars in extra interest to your lender. And to you.

Bottom line: It pays to do the calculations if you're shopping around for a mortgage. You may find that the effective rate offered by one lender is actually higher than that offered by another — even though it may appear lower.

"The key is the amortization schedule. With it, you can create some mortgage magic of your own," says Ron Cirotto of Different Products in Burlington. His company has created a special mortgage software program called *Morgij2*, which will help you figure out the best approach to paying off your mortgage. *Morgij2* comes in two versions — a heavy-duty DOS version for professionals (mortgage brokers, real estate lawyers, etc.), which costs $95; and a user-friendly Windows version designed for novice users, which costs $39.

Cirotto likes one strategy in particular, which makes effective use of the amortization schedule. The first column in this schedule is the principal amount, which must be paid back in full.

You have no say in this. Where you do have flexibility is in the second column — the amount of interest you pay with each monthly payment. If, for example, you were to take your current month's payment and add to it the principal portion of the following month's payment, you'd save the interest on this amount not only next month but also every month thereafter. Doing this just once will literally put hundreds of dollars in your pocket. If you repeat this process once every year, the savings can run into thousands of dollars.

Let's look at a $100,000 mortgage with an interest rate of 7.5% and amortized over 25 years to show you what I mean. If you take the current month's payment of $615.45 and add to it the principal portion of next month's payment of $116.81 and pay the total amount — $731.26 — when you make your payment this month, you'll save $614.74 over the life of the mortgage.

That's 5.3 times the $116.81 principal prepayment you made, or a return of 530% on your investment. Plus — and this is another crucial point — you'll be doing so with after-tax dollars. If you're in a 50% tax bracket, that $116 prepayment actually represents a 1,060% return in pre-tax dollars.

To make this strategy work, you must have an open mortgage. This is just another reason why most of us are better off with an open, short-term, variable-rate mortgage. If you don't have an open mortgage, look at the totals under each of the columns in the amortization schedule. Add up all the principal portions of your second-year payments and prepay that amount along with your 12th payment. (Most mortgages will permit you to pay down your principal by 15% a year.) In this case above, the 12 monthly payments would run to $1,401.72. By using this strategy, the second year of the amortization schedule effectively disappears.

"This concept, by the way, has been known since 450 BC when the usury laws were revised in Jerusalem," observes Cirotto. "It's just that not too many people talk about it. Certainly lenders don't."

While you're at it, he advises, ask your lender whether you have what is known as a monthly pay mortgage with an "exact day interest factor." Some mortgage lenders use the exact number of days in each month to calculate the monthly interest factor. This is important to you as a borrower because it means you'll be paying a higher effective rate than if the lender based his calculations on a 360-day year. So ask. It's worth your time.

Best approach? Go weekly, says Cirotto. It's the only way to fly. Once you decide to do this, ask your lender for the amount of your monthly payment and, if you decide to pay weekly, tell him or her you want to divide that payment by four. This will accelerate the payment process and save you the most money. All major banks, he notes, offer weekly repayment options.

A final word about the importance of knowing the effective interest rate you're paying on your mortgage, especially in the context of using mortgage funds for investment purposes. Without this knowledge, you really can't determine the real return on any investment you might make.

Keep yourself in the driver's seat

If you're in the process of renewing your mortgage, do not, under any circumstances, accept the first rate offered by your lender.

Ask for a better rate — unless it's really rock bottom — and ask for it in writing. Tell your lender before you sign that you want to check what the competition is offering. I guarantee you'll get a better rate.

If your mortgage is coming up for renewal in 1998 — and you're concerned where rates will be in a year's time — think about cutting a deal now. Go to your bank. Explain that you're already a customer, that you believe rates will be lower in 1998, and that you're prepared to lock in now for five years — if the bank will shave another half-point from today's rate. Some will.

However, if you believe, as I do, that rates will drop further, you might be better off waiting another six months before taking action. That's a good strategy, even if your mortgage is coming up for renewal now. You may be able to lock in at an even better rate. Whatever the case, the closer you get to the time, the more accommodating your lender will be.

Chapter 6

School Days Don't Have to Mean School Daze

The tax collector must love poor people.
He's trying to create so many.

Should you buy a house for a student?

College and university fees have been rising in recent years — but they're not the real culprit in a student's budget. The big killer is living costs — and that's often what parents resent the most because they feel they're at the mercy of landlords in many college towns.

There is a solution, of course. You can join the landlords and, in the process, provide subsidized housing for your son or daughter and perhaps even profit yourself at the end of the day.

Where to start? First, take a few minutes and tally up the cost of a university education. Break out the costs for living expenses. A big chunk of that, you can be sure, goes for rent. If you multiply that figure by four or five, you'll have a pretty good idea of how much money you'll have at your disposal to pay for the mortgage, utilities, and other expenses. The next step is to come up with the down payment.

It doesn't matter, as far as Revenue Canada is concerned, that you intend to rent part of this property to your son or daughter. To Revenue Canada, it's just a normal real estate transaction, in which you'll be able to claim all the interest you pay on mortgages and loans associated with the property as a tax deduction plus all maintenance, insurance, utilities, upkeep, etc. — perhaps even capital cost allowance (depreciation) if you're making a profit.

Then there's the salary for a property manager, which is the norm in rental situations with a number of tenants. There is no reason why this could not be your daughter. After all, she will be managing and maintaining your investment — and therein lies an interesting tax twist.

The salary you pay your child will be a tax deduction to you but will probably not be taxable in her hands because she would not have earned enough from a summer or part-time job to produce taxable income.

Even if she has enough income to be taxable, your daughter will still be able to claim her tuition and a full-time student credit. That may be enough to reduce her taxable income to zero, even to get her back on side as a dependent exemption.

Many taxpayers often miss out by failing to claim rental expenses when their rental income reaches zero. That's a mistake, because we can claim negative rental income as a deduction against our regular salary — even though the reason for this was due in part to the salary paid to our son or daughter.

In time, real estate tends to rise in value. In the case of rental real estate, the capital gain is taxable only when you sell the property. To reduce this liability, you might consider putting the property in the name of your son or daughter, who will then be able to claim it as a principal residence. Upon graduation, your child could then sell the property and give the proceeds back to you — or use the money as a down payment on a new residence when he or she finally does go to work. It's a great head start. In this example, a condo might be a better bet because it would require less maintenance.

Whatever the case, it's a great education in real estate and starting to think in multi-dimensional terms.

RESPs are better than ever

Registered Education Savings Plans — or RESPs, as they are known in the industry — got a big boost in the 1997 budget, but they still may not be the best alternative for your money.

Under the new rules, the annual contribution limit has been raised to $4,000 — with a lifetime maximum of $42,000 per student. While there is no tax deduction for these contributions, any income earned inside the plan is allowed to compound tax-free. Over two decades, this can represent quite a tidy sum.

The new limits effectively allow taxpayers to accelerate the process. Given the rising cost of education — and the very real prospect of significantly higher tuition costs down the road, driven by even greater government funding cutbacks — these changes make a lot of sense.

Another key change: If your child decides not to pursue post-secondary education, you'll be able to transfer your RESP funds to your RRSP — assuming, of course, you have enough contribution room.

Most people, however, would be better off contributing to their RRSP and using the tax rebate for the RESP — a far more effective multi-dimensional strategy.

Even then, it may not make sense to buy an off-the-shelf RESP. Historically, Registered Education Savings Plans have tended to invest their assets in interest-bearing investments. This was fine when interest rates produced double-digit returns, but with rates at 40-year lows, these plans are not likely to make much of a dent in tuition fees in coming years.

There are two alternatives that may provide a better solution: one is to simply invest money in mutual funds or stocks in your child's name; the second is to enrol in a self-directed RESP.

In the case of the first option — buying mutual funds in your child's name — you will need to consider the impact of attribution rules on your tax return. Under these rules, any interest or dividends earned by these investments must be declared on your tax return, even though they are held in your child's name.

Capital gains are treated differently. These are taxed in your child's name. If your child is under 18, there is every prospect that he or she will not be taxed at all. The trick then is to invest this money into growth mutual funds or stocks whose primary focus is to produce capital gains.

The second option — a self-directed RESP — offers more flexibility than commercial-type plans. These are available through independent financial planners and offer a wide range of investment options, including mutual funds and stocks. In addition, you can even change beneficiaries. That includes naming yourself as beneficiary.

Once your child turns 18 — or even as he approaches 18 — a different set of tax rules comes into play that will enable you to adopt an alternative strategy. Suppose, for example, you give your child $50,000 instead, which he invests in a solid blue-chip equity fund that earns 10% or $5,000 a year, or even as much as 15% or $7,500 a year.

That $7,500 would be earned as dividends and capital gains, which would be taxed at an attractive rate in the child's name. Now, if you invested that $50,000 instead and the $7,500 in earnings were in your name, you'd wind up paying half of it back to the government, leaving you with about only $4,000 to help you with your child's education costs. By giving the money to your child to invest in his name, you effectively cut out the middleman.

Do student RRSPs make sense?

It depends. In most cases, I would say *no* — but if you've earned enough where an RRSP contribution would make a real difference in your taxable income, it may be a wise move.

In most cases, however, students don't earn enough to make an RRSP contribution worthwhile. A better choice is to carry forward your allowable RRSP contribution and use it later when you've completed your education and are in the labour force.

In recent years, your RRSP limit has been set at 18% of your previous year's earned income. What's important is that this contribution is cumulative and can now be carried forward indefinitely, thanks to the 1997 budget.

If, for example, you put $1,000 into your RRSP, you might save $100 in taxes while still in school. The same $1,000 carried forward to after graduation could be worth $400 or more in tax savings. If carried forward over a four- or five-year period, the cumulative tax savings could be quite substantial.

That's why filing a tax return is important — even though the student may have little or no taxable income. This way Revenue Canada is able to track unused RRSP contributions, which can be used later when the student has a larger tax liability.

If, however, as a student you use the money you were prepared to put into your RRSP — and invest it in mutual funds outside your RRSP — you'll get virtually the same tax-free compounding you would enjoy inside your RRSP, because your taxable income is either nil or very, very low.

In essence, you're really putting your money away today — not in your RRSP, but in a mutual fund that can be flipped later into your RRSP, where the tax relief is much greater. Until then, a student who earns less than $6,500 a year will enjoy tax-free compounding. As a matter of strategy, you should think about declaring any capital gains earned every year. This way, you will have tax-free money to put inside your RRSP down the road.

There are times, however, when I do recommend that a student take full advantage of RRSP provisions. Here I'm talking about benefits to the parent rather than to the student. It's the student's income that determines whether he or she is a tax deduction for the parent.

This applies equally to supporting spouses. Many spouses who lost their jobs in the recession have gone back to school full-time.

If the student has slightly more than $2,500 in net income, for example, she is diminished as a tax deduction. If she is able to put some of this money into an RRSP, she would effectively lower her income to a point where she is once again a dependant for her parents or spouse.

Here the parent or spouse is effectively getting the tax relief at his or her marginal rate, which will be substantially higher. If necessary, a parent or spouse should consider putting money into the student's RRSP — if it would lower the student's earned income to a point where the parent or spouse can again use the student as a tax deduction. If the student's income is reduced to zero, the parent is also able to transfer the tuition and full-time student deduction over to the parent's tax return. So, it's probably a trade-off for the parent.

A student who earns $10,000, for example, only has to pay tax on $3,500. By making use of the tuition tax deduction and putting $2,000 into an RRSP, the student might be able to eliminate his or her tax liability entirely. The big reason for buying an RRSP at this stage in the child's life is to take full advantage of the magic of compounding, which can become quite significant in later years.

Here the parent or spouse is effectively getting the tax relief at his or her marginal rate, which will be substantially higher.

Your children can start on their way by taking all the bits of money they get at Christmas, in child tax benefits, etc. and putting it away until you have enough to buy a CSB, a term deposit, or a GIC.

Personally, I prefer investing the money in a mutual fund. You can start the ball rolling with as little as $500 and build on this by investing small amounts through a monthly purchase plan.

Best choice? A growth fund. Simply because it will produce the best returns over an 18- or 20-year period.

If your child is newborn, that's how long it will be before he or she will need the money. Forget about what that fund does today or tomorrow. If it's down from time to time, think of it as a good opportunity to buy more units than usual under the monthly savings plan.

The investment, however, must be made in your name — no matter what type you buy. In terms of tax, the thing Revenue Canada will look at is the attribution rule, which asks, *Whose money is it?*

If you give your child money, for example, Revenue Canada will rule that it's your money, and you, not your child, will have to pay tax on it.

If it's the child's own money, however, and you can document that, then there will be no attribution. This is especially the case if the money is derived from the child benefit program, which is clearly meant for the use of the child. At the same time, there's no limit on the amount of money you can give to your child. And providing the money is not put in a revenue-producing investment, you will not be taxed on this income.

If, for example, you gave your child an allowance of $10 a week or $520 a year, you'd have to earn approximately $1,000 to have $520 in after-tax income to pay for the allowance. On the other hand, if you had $10,000 in an investment that earned $1,000 a year and gave that to your child, you would have to pay tax on that $1,000 because of the attribution rule.

But only once. After that the $1,000 would be your child's, and at 10% that $1,000 would earn $100 for him. This $100 would be taxed at your child's rate. This would probably be 0% because he would not likely earn more than $6,500. That's the amount we're all able to earn before having to pay tax. Next year that $10,000 will produce another $1,000. Again, you'll have to pay tax on the amount. But only once.

Now your child has $2,000 on which he can earn $200 a year. Repeat the process for a few years, and your child will be able to have $800 or $1,000 a year coming in. Great for your son or daughter, and at no cost to you.

You can, of course, take back the $10,000 at this point, but you may find it worthwhile sharing your money with your family rather than with the tax collector.

How to get the government to pay for your child's education

Having the government foot the bill for your son's or daughter's education is a question of making attribution rules work in your favour and tapping in to the advantages of a Systematic Withdrawal Plan.

We normally think of Systematic Withdrawal Plans as a tax-efficient way to supplement retirement income, but they can also be used to fund your child's education.

Here's what I mean: Suppose you were to give your child $50,000 and he invests it in a Systematic Withdrawal Plan, from which he takes out $500 a month or $6,000 a year.

It's better to have the income in your child's name than in yours for two reasons: withdrawals are tax-free, and there is no attribution in the case of capital gains. If there is attribution, it would be on the interest and dividend income, which, in any case, would be very small.

That's, of course, if your child is under 18 years of age. If he is over 18, all investment income is attributed to his name.

Bottom line: Your child has $6,000 worth of income, but very little of it must be declared. And with a bit of planning, you may also be able to keep your child's taxable income down to zero. This will enable you to transfer his education and full-time student deduction to your tax return. In the final analysis, you'll probably make more in tax rebates than you would had you invested the $50,000 in your name.

By taking a multi-dimensional approach, you get the government to at least share in the cost of your child's education.

While most mutual fund companies offer Systematic Withdrawal Plans, two of the companies that have made a big thing about it are Templeton and Trimark. Both have plenty of statistical information to show you what happens to your investment. It always makes interesting reading.

If you had invested that $50,000, for example, in Templeton Growth in 1977 and withdrew $182,141 over the next 20 years, your $50,000 investment would be worth $329,041 today — and that's after all withdrawals.

If you had invested $50,000 in Trimark Fund in September 1981, your investment would have grown to $626,430 by the end of 1996 — even though you withdrew $155,550 over the 15-year period.

Are student travel expenses tax deductible?

Not only are student travel expenses deductible, but tuition costs are as well. In order to claim these deductions, you must satisfy Revenue Canada on three counts:

* The student must be attending a postsecondary educational institution.

* The student must have a job at his or her new location.

* The new residence must be at least 40 kilometres closer to this new job.

The last two conditions must be met in order for the student to claim travel expenses. These include the cost of travel (air/train or even use of a car, including gasoline, hotel meals, meals en route).

These also include, by the way, travelling home from a post-secondary educational institution. This can be far greater than just travel expense, including also the cost of breaking leases or even getting out of utility contracts. That's because the student is coming home — not to live with her parents — but to get a summer job. These expenses are valuable because they can be used to lower taxable income.

This could be an important point if the student had a summer job or other income, such as a bursary or scholarship, where she now has taxable income. The first $500 of any award, by the way, is tax-free.

The child's taxable income must be at "zero" in order for you to transfer her tuition and full-time student deduction to your tax return. That may mean some additional tax planning for your child. If she has earned income in 1996, it may be worth your while to contribute to an RRSP for her so that you can claim her full-time student deductions.

A fine point: If you go back to school and you don't have a full-time job, you will not qualify for moving expenses. In the case of a part-time job, your moving expenses may be disallowed because the rules state your move must be to a full-time job.

Chapter 7

What to Do When Your Job Comes to an End

A recession is where the other guy loses his job.
A depression is where you lose your job.
And panic is where your wife loses hers.

Moving on

What to do if you lose your job really depends on your age, health, and financial position. Essentially, there are three options:

★ Take your severance and go into retirement.

★ Roll the severance money into an RRSP and find another job.

★ Go into business for yourself.

For most people, the only real option is finding another job —
and how well they do depends in large measure on the attitudes
they bring with them.

Whatever you do, don't overreact. You really have to under-
stand that you must go through a grieving process, says Colleen
Quinn, a partner with career-management consultants Bond &
Partners, in Toronto.

"Where you'll be in even three or four weeks from that time
will be a very different place. Give yourself permission to go
through this process — and see it as an opportunity to take the
time to refocus and think through what you want to do with
your next job and what you want your next work environment
to look like."

The biggest problem, most often, is well-meaning friends who
come out of the woodwork to tell you about this opportunity or
that. It's a normal knee-jerk reaction to go, go, go, but more often
than not, says Quinn, the chances of making a poor decision —
and failing in your next position — are high.

"If you don't allow yourself time to get rid of the negative
feelings, any lingering bitterness you may harbour can creep into
your job interviews and, when you do land a position, make it
difficult for you to settle in and bond with your new company."
People, however, do eventually move on, whether they're prepared to or not, says Quinn. "Part of that preparation is this
grieving process and reconnecting with ourselves and focusing
on our dreams and aspirations, which we often lose sight of while
trying to earn a living."

We should also use this period, Quinn urges, to get back in
touch with our value systems. This is important because we're
most likely to be successful and make our greatest contribution
in companies and organizations that have value systems similar
to our own.

"A job or work environment in itself isn't dissatisfying, but an
environment where our values, attitudes, and beliefs come in

conflict with those of the organization can be very destructive to our self-esteem and self-confidence. It's hard to be the best you can be in this kind of environment."

The first rule is to know yourself. Initially, people will tell you that they do. But they don't. That's critical. Step back and get in touch with yourself and find out what you want to do with your life and the kind of job that's in tune with your values. It may well not be in the career you're in now.

"That's one of the reasons why you should not use your last position as a launching point to your next job," explains Quinn. "Also take the time to step back and understand the learned behaviours you've picked up along the way — what you've been taught about success and failure and the emotional/behaviour drivers in your life."

"That includes what you enjoy. A lot of people," adds Quinn, "do well in careers they may not really enjoy or necessarily excel in."

Negotiating your severance package

No matter what you're offered, ask for time to think it over, and under no circumstances sign anything until you do. In most instances, there's room to negotiate, according to Toronto lawyer Tom Kravanis.

"It's very rare that an employer will say, *This is it, take it or leave it, and if you leave it, we'll fight you all the way.* Even in those rare circumstances," says Kravanis, "there may be a little flexibility from the employer — even where there had been no flexibility before — when he or she is faced with the possibility of litigation. Instead of paying money to outside counsel, it's often cheaper for an employer to sweeten the pot enough to cut a deal. Everyone benefits, including the employer. Often, it helps to maintain goodwill among remaining employees."

Usual package: There are many factors that come into play, but a rough guide is one month for every year of employment. Factors that tend to change this equation include the employee's age — the older you are, for example, the less likely you are to find a comparable job.

There have been cases where damages have been awarded to employees for mental distress and where employers have been particularly harsh in the treatment of staff.

"You should also request — and expect — a letter of reference from the employer as well as an agreement from the employer not to give a negative reference in any follow-up telephone calls," says Kravanis.

A severance package should not be limited to a financial settlement, says career-management consultant Colleen Quinn.

"Ideally, a severance package should represent a reimbursement of a realistic time period of what it would take for an individual to get another job. Many people lose sight of that. They see it essentially as financial, but it is also about career management and keeping them whole during the process — so that they can focus specifically on what to do with their careers."

That's why out-placement/career counselling is usually a non-negotiable part of the severance package.

Option 1: Take the money and run
. . . when retirement makes sense

Retirement can make a lot of sense, if you're in your late 50s or early 60s and you have extra income from your company to bridge the gaps until your pension kicks in. If you decide on this option, your first concern is what to do with your severance or retirement allowance.

Ideally, you should attempt to shelter as much of this allowance as possible.

How much of your retirement allowance or severance can you roll into your RRSP? Under current rules, you can invest $2,000 for every year you worked at the company. If the allowance or award is $60,000, for example, and you had worked at this company for 22 years, you would be able to shelter $44,000 and only be required to pay tax on the remaining $16,000. The difference in your tax-payable using this strategy — $8,000 vs. $22,000.

The $2,000 rollover privilege was capped in 1995 and no longer applies to years of service after that date. However, if your company did not have a pension plan during this period, you can roll over an extra $1,500 a year into your RRSP for every year worked until 1989.

This kind of complexity is why it's important to have a financial planner assist you with the eventual direction of your money.

There is another question many people are wrestling with today. If you have the option of taking a buy-out, should you do so now or wait until the next window? In most cases, that window can be three or five years down the road.

Here are a few factors to consider:

* Is there a possibility you may be caught in another corporate downsizing — before being able to opt for the next package?

* Is the financial health of your company a concern? If it is, you might be better off taking the buy-out now and letting the insurance company that handles your company's pension worry about that.

* Also, don't forget that the $2,000 rollover allowance, as noted earlier, has been capped as of 1995. If you decide to opt for retirement five years from now, this deduction will not be available to you for 1996, 1997, 1998, 1999, and 2000.

These are real concerns and require a lot of hard thinking. But if you decide to go now, your best option is to shelter as much of your severance as possible. It will pay off handsomely down the road — when you will need it most.

Option 2: Find another job — what do you do with your pension?

If you decide to look for another job, looking after your pension has to be one of the first things you should look at to avoid potential tax problems. Many Canadians mistakenly believe they cannot roll any of their pensions into their RRSPs. That is not true.

If your pension is being wound down or you expect to receive a lump sum payout from your pension, these amounts can still be rolled over directly to your RRSP. The trick is to make sure you don't touch this money on the way through. You can do this simply by empowering the institution where you have your RRSP to go after the pension fund on your behalf. This will enable you to transfer the money in your pension directly to your RRSP without any tax consequences. It's simply a transfer from one trustee to another.

Whatever you do, do not take this money yourself. If you do, it will be classed as ordinary income by Revenue Canada, and only 18% of your earned income, to a maximum of $13,500 (plus any unused contribution room), can be contributed to your RRSP.

It's also important for you to learn and apply all the rules properly. If you don't, you could lose as much as half of your money.

But even if you follow the rules, there is a possible glitch. There always is. It's called the Alternative Minimum Tax, or AMT as it is known. When we have an unusual jump in income in one year, we can trigger AMT even though we transferred this money into our RRSP. However, if this is a one-time jump and your income levels out in coming years, you should be able to recoup the AMT you paid.

It may also be possible to ease this tax problem by talking to your employer. In some cases, you might even be able to spread your settlement over this year and next. This strategy may keep you from being bumped into a higher tax bracket — and if you use the rollovers we've been discussing, you may not have to worry about AMT at all.

The drawback to this strategy — you aren't able to get at your money as quickly and won't be able to earn as much on it as a result. An alternative is to get your employer to pay you interest on these funds between the time you get the first instalment and the second on the following January. Your employer may also like the idea. After all, the company will have use of this money during the period.

I'm frequently asked by people why they should roll this money into their RRSPs if they're going to need some of it to live on in a few months' time. The answer is simple — to save taxes.

If you roll all this money into your RRSP now, it will keep you from being bumped into a higher tax bracket. Also, the money will be able to grow in a tax-free environment. And if you want money, you can always remove it a bit at a time — usually when your taxable income is very low. If you remove $5,000 or less at a time, the institution will withhold 10% for tax purposes. If you take out $15,000, the withholding tax jumps to 20%, and beyond that the withholding tax rises to 30%.

In addition, you will have to add these withdrawals to your taxable income and pay tax on the total when you file your return. In the meantime, you'll be earning income on the remainder tax-free inside your RRSP. In the long run, you'll have a more prosperous retirement.

Option 3: Go into business for yourself

Starting up one's own business has a lot of emotional appeal and is becoming attractive to an increasing number of Canadians who are looking for ways to insulate themselves against layoffs. Witness the sharp increase in home businesses in recent years and the growing trend by corporations to contract out services that were once done in-house. Other Canadians are turning to franchising for the answer.

But going into business for yourself does not necessarily solve future employment problems or make you rich. There are pitfalls, even with franchises, and these must be weighed carefully before you make a final decision. Above all, know what you're getting into and what the odds are for your success.

Let's take a close look at franchising.

Franchising: Entrepreneurs need not apply

You'd think it would be the exact opposite. But it isn't — there's a lot of anecdotal evidence to suggest that entrepreneurs make lousy franchisees.

There are exceptions, of course, but the best candidates are those with strong managerial and communication skills — above all, people who are prepared to toe the line and follow the franchiser's directions to the letter. If you are — and you've picked the right franchise — there's a good chance you'll succeed.

Entrepreneurial types find franchises very restraining and confining, says John Sotos, a partner with the Toronto law firm of Sotos Kravanis who has been advising franchisers and franchisees for the past 18 years. Even if they do well, adds Sotos, they eventually get restless and begin to resent the franchiser and the franchiser's dictates as to how the system should be run.

At some point, entrepreneurs get the feeling that they know

more than the franchiser and could do better on their own. Generally, if they're unhappy, they don't do well.

If you are entrepreneurial and like the franchise concept, think about becoming a franchiser instead. You'll probably do better. The skill set is different — more in keeping with the entrepreneur's special strengths. Here these skills work in his or her favour.

For most people, however, the only real option is buying a franchise. The best is one with a proven, successful system that requires the franchise to follow a number of preordained steps and procedures that have demonstrated a high success rate.

This is where many people make their greatest mistake, says Sotos, who has guided hundreds of prospective franchisees through the process. They see franchising in terms of proven, successful systems like McDonald's or Midas and associate that image with a start-up outfit that hasn't even sold its first franchise. That's a crucial point. In the case of new franchises, you don't have a successful system. They're unproven and often include inexperienced management or a system without the financial resources behind it to make it successful.

Strong management is critical. Ideally, the people behind the franchise should have strong industry experience and have a team in place to assist you with marketing, store operations, and site selection. Ability to administer the franchise's advertising fund in a professional manner is essential. These funds should be segregated from the franchiser's other funds. Saying that the fund exists, without evidence that it does, or how it is administered, is not good enough, Sotos stresses.

These points are givens. But if you don't have these resources at your disposal, how can you get the support you need? And you will need this help. One of the main reasons people choose franchising over building a business from scratch is that they are able to tap into a mass-marketing program they could not otherwise create on their own — in essence, take advantage of the brand recognition a national franchise offers.

The other main reason: to take advantage of volume purchasing. This is important because it gives the franchisee a competitive edge. If the franchiser does not have this advantage — or is not prepared to offer it — I would very seriously question whether you should buy that franchise.

Typically, people who buy franchises are going into business for the first time. They still think as consumers and don't always value professional advice. These individuals can't find ready employment in their fields, and deep down they always had a yen to go into business for themselves. Usually, says Sotos, they go into something they enjoy — not a bad thing in itself — but the problem is that they go into the franchise with a romanticized image of what is involved. That's why so many go for bar and restaurant franchises. The reality of being an owner/operator of a bar or restaurant, however, is totally different from that of being a patron. In most instances, the people who go into these franchises are not really prepared for the long hours, the high staff turnover, and the customer-relations problems. The result — usually failure.

The other big pitfall — people simply fail to do their homework. No one, says Sotos, should buy a franchise unless he or she has it vetted by experienced franchise professionals. That includes lawyers, accountants, and bankers with a solid background in franchising — people who have seen it all before and who can show you where the pitfalls are.

You should expect them to walk you through the process and use their experience to show you what you can expect from the franchise agreement you'll be asked to sign and what, particularly, stands out as unusual.

An agreement, notes Sotos, that front-end loads all fees and/or gives the franchiser the right to force-feed merchandise on the franchisee has the potential for abuse — and that's what usually happens.

Once people understand, in plain English, what's involved — as opposed to the typical platitudes you see in many of these contracts — they are able to make a decision with their eyes wide open and with no surprises at the end of the road. If you go through the financials with an accountant who understands all the ins and outs of franchising and discover, for example, that the expenses outlined in the pro forma statements are understated to the extent that the franchise is likely to generate a loss, you won't be as eager to buy that franchise.

Bottom line: Before you sign anything, get advice. The best you can buy. It's much, much less expensive than losing $250,000, and it will save all the family discord, including marriage breakdown, that often follows in the wake of a financial loss of this size. There's more at stake than just the money you're putting up, warn experts like Sotos. If you're in your mid-50s and lose your family as well as your savings, it's a devastating experience many individuals find hard to recover from.

Legal costs for this kind of advice can run anywhere between $1,500 to $5,000, depending on the complexity of the franchise agreement. Don't let that stop you, even if the franchiser tells you that he or she won't change the agreement to meet concerns from your lawyer. That may or may not be the case — but if you're putting up $250,000, you really should know what you're getting into and what your chances for success are.

No matter what the franchiser tells you, says Sotos, most franchise agreements are negotiable. So don't go in with the approach that the franchiser won't budge. In most cases, changes can be made — to your territory or even to some of the financial terms. If the franchise is a new system, you can probably negotiate a longer term without ponying up extra money. Or be able to keep the same royalties when the contract comes up for renewal. If you don't try, you'll never know.

As a rule, the more established the franchise, the fewer the changes you'll be able to make. If the franchise is a proven success, the franchiser will be less likely to allow you to tinker with the formula.

This is especially important if you're buying a new franchise. In many of these cases, the franchise agreement may be full of holes. Don't assume that franchisers always know what they're doing. They also make mistakes. In some cases, their franchise agreements are adapted from other franchise contracts and are little more than a composite of these agreements rather than an agreement unique to the needs of the particular franchise, or they may not take into consideration your strengths, weaknesses, and philosophy.

Note: Once you sign on the dotted line, you will not be able to make changes later.

Given the potential for misunderstanding and for abuse, you would think a lot of these agreements would wind up in the courts. Some do, says Sotos, but most franchisees have mortgaged their homes and invested their life savings in the venture and have very few resources left to take their case to the courts.

While all this may sound negative, there are also a number of stunning success stories in franchising. It's a great way to do business — if you have the right ingredients in place and you buy the right franchise, one with a distinctive trade name, a competitive advantage, solid training and retraining programs, as well as an ongoing monitoring system to help keep franchisees on track.

Here's a partial list of some of the things you should expect before laying down a cent on a franchise no matter how great the opportunity sounds in the franchiser's advertising:

* An established, proven, and highly successful system in place.

* A marketing program to promote the franchise.

* Careful selection of potential franchisees. In some instances, the only qualification is having the money to put up. Candidates should fit the franchiser's profile.

* Training and retraining programs.

* Regular inspections — and timely advice to franchisees where they have fallen short.

* Effective reporting and accounting systems — so that the franchisee knows when his or her costs are out of line and how to correct any mistakes. Good franchisers also have established profiles of candidates who are most likely to succeed. There are essentially two types of successful candidates: those who feel comfortable and who are prepared to follow dictated mandates (business is increasingly complex, and you need someone who is not going to resist a proven success formula), and those with people and communication skills.

Financing: Make sure you do your homework first

If you don't do your financing homework, your banker will insist that you do. Before any money changes hands, he or she will want to make sure that you've investigated the franchise from head to toe — and that you fully understand the nature of the franchise, especially how much support or lack of support you can expect from the franchiser.

Dan Farmer, senior manager, national franchise market, for the Royal Bank of Canada, suggests you do a lot of tire-kicking before you make up your mind. That includes talking to other franchisees in that system. "We want you to know what you're getting into. It's not in our interests — or in the interests of the franchiser — to have you fail."

Many leading franchisers, he notes, have designed national banking packages with one of the major banks. In these cases, that bank already has a good understanding of the franchise, how it operates, and its potential.

What does the bank look for? "Management expertise, experience, energy, drive, and commitment. You can sense it almost immediately. We look for past examples where the individual has demonstrated these qualities," says Farmer.

How much will the bank finance? That depends on the franchise — the size and health of the system as well as the sector it's playing in. There's no simple formula. In most cases, no formula at all. As a rule, the bank will expect you to put up 25% to 30%, but even that figure, adds Farmer, can be tailored to the individual and the franchise itself. A highly profitable system with a successful track record will obviously require less.

In fact, the equity-to-loan ratio used by the bank for a particular franchise could be viewed as a criterion of the kind of risk you might be undertaking.

Guarantees could also be involved, but they, too, depend on the track record of the franchise. If you expect 100% financing, you can assume that some form of guarantee will be involved.

Bottom line: Surround yourself with franchise-friendly professionals — lawyers, accountants, and bankers — and leverage their advice. Ideally, you should tap into a network of professionals who have dealt with each other before and who can work together with you and the franchiser.

The bank will want to know you're getting the best advice you can.

Also worth noting: When you're buying a franchise, you're really buying someone else's mistakes and the knowledge that has come from them — without having to go through the pain.

What about using your severance to finance a new business?

Using your severance for financing sounds great, at least at first glance, when you're scrambling for money to start a new business or finance a franchise — but it may not be your best option.

If you do, you'll lose half of your severance to the tax collector. Unless it is sheltered, the award will be added to your income in the year it is received and taxed at your full marginal rate. In most instances, that will be 53%.

A far better strategy would be to roll as much of this allowance into a self-directed RRSP and focus on using that money for your retirement. Once taken out, it cannot be put back later. So think long and hard. It really isn't your best option.

A better approach would be to take out a new mortgage on your home and use these funds to finance your new business. This way, the interest on your mortgage now becomes tax deductible, and you'll win both ways — you'll be able to escape taxation on a big chunk of your retirement allowance, and you'll have a tax-deductible mortgage that can be written off against your business as interest on a business loan.

Chapter 8

Are You Ready
for Retirement?

Never put off until tomorrow what you can do today.
There probably will be a higher tax on it.

Start planning for your retirement now

You'd be surprised how many people aren't prepared for their retirements. I see a lot of worried faces at seminars these days — people who are approaching their retirement years and are suddenly aware that they are running out of time. Virtually all are looking for magic solutions, knowing deep down there aren't any and that, if anything, the noose will become a bit tighter as universal programs fall by the wayside.

If you're in this position, there are still a few things you can do to get off on the right foot. If you're within five years of retirement, start planning seriously now. You'll need that time to put yourself in a position to take advantage of all the options open to you.

First step: Put your financial house in order. That includes paying off all your debt — or at least as much as you can — and developing a realistic retirement budget that covers your basic needs, leaving a bit of room for inflation.

Second step: Look at the projected cash flow available to you in retirement and develop an investment strategy that will produce the income you'll need to match your retirement needs.

In most cases, that means coming to terms with your risk tolerance. That's a toughie. Most people will tell you that they understand market volatility, that they can handle a market correction — at least until there's a major sell-off. Then emotions run amok, and all the best-laid plans in the world go right out the window. Make sure this doesn't happen to you. It can make a big difference in how you'll live in retirement.

There are two ways to deal with this:

* First, understand how much risk you can really handle emotionally. That's critical if you want to avoid mistakes later on. That means putting your money in investments that won't keep you awake at night when things go wrong. And they will.

* Second, and perhaps even more important, understand how markets work and how to use a carefully crafted multi-dimensional investment strategy that not only reduces risk but also provides a consistent, superior rate of return year after year.

Third step: Maximize your RRSP contributions during the years you have left. If you still have unused contribution room, borrow if you need to, but make those contributions.

This will do two things. It will help to reduce your taxes while you're still working and enable you to amass a greater nest egg inside your RRSP that will compound on a tax-free basis. The sooner you do this, the more you'll have to take out every year in your retirement. Even three or four years can make a huge difference. In most cases, you should be able to repay this easily over the next five years.

This brings up another point. Risk tolerance. There was a time when you could earn quite respectable double-digit returns from fixed-income investments like GICs. But those glory days are long past, and if we want to maximize our retirement income, we really have no option but to include stocks as part of our investment mix. I say "no option" because if we don't — given today's low-interest rate environment — we will most certainly outlive our money. And these conditions are not likely to change anytime soon.

If you've been a GIC investor, take the opportunity to learn about time and risk. As a general rule, stocks not only outperform investments like GICs but also do so consistently — and at virtually no risk — if held over a long period.

How long? At least five years. A recent study on investment returns by Scotia Capital Markets shows that in no five-year period during the past 35 years have equities lost money. That's not all. It also shows that equities outperformed fixed-income investments, including GICs, for 25 of the 35 years reviewed in this study. The only time they didn't was during the 1980s, when interest rates skyrocketed to historic highs in the Western world.

Add this to the fact that people are living longer and that they will require income for at least 22 years. Without the kind of returns generated by stocks, most people simply won't make it — if they rely on GIC-type investments.

The best way to reach your goals is through a balanced portfolio that includes growth as well as blue-chip equity funds, bonds, and foreign investments. By adjusting the mix, you can reduce or increase the volatility — and returns — in keeping with your risk tolerance, enabling you to use a multi-dimensional strategy to the maximum.

This brings up another problem faced by many people who use a number of funds in their RRIFs. The more funds you own, the more paperwork is involved, especially in arranging and keeping track of monthly or quarterly payments from each of the funds. The simplest way to handle this is to consolidate your holdings into three or four key funds. Another way is to put your assets into a wrap account like Mackenzie's Star and AGF's Harmony Programs. In both of these programs, you'll be able to achieve all the diversification you'll ever need but at a risk level you can accept and earning returns consistent with this risk. All this — plus only one fund to deal with.

Retirement planning is more than making "smart" investments. It also requires a lot of planning and, above all, time to make it happen. Far too many people start the process too late. And when they do, they are confronted, more often than not, with the realization that they may outlive their money — unless they make significant contributions to their RRSPs every year until they retire. In many instances, this is money they don't have.

Take the case of a 41-year-old who has $60,000 in her RRSP and who would like to retire at age 60 on $4,000 a month until she's 85. Assuming a 3% annual inflation rate, she will need $7,014 a month 19 years from now just to match today's buying power.

If that $60,000 earns 10% a year, this individual will need to invest $10,945 a year for the next 19 years to create an investment pool to provide this income.

The 45-year-old who expects to retire on $3,000 a month from his company pension will also face a funding crunch. Unless indexed, that $3,000 a month will only have the purchasing power of $1,674 in today's dollars.

For this individual, who has $40,000 in his RRSP, to retire on $4,000 a month in today's dollars, he will need to invest an extra $6,132 a year. Finding this money every year is not easy, especially for parents facing postsecondary education costs in the near future.

Yet these are crucial years for these investors who stand to lose heavily down the road when they reach retirement. A $10,000 investment that earns 10% a year will be worth $67,275 in 20 years' time.

That's what's on the line every time you fail to make an RRSP contribution or to take full advantage of your RRSP contribution room.

Investing in GICs and term deposits — as long as they fail to earn at least 10% a year — is also counterproductive. There is no way you can reach your retirement goals by putting your money in an investment that not only fails to meet your return targets but also offers no prospect of capital gain, which must be a prime consideration with every investment you make.

That's why I prefer mutual funds. Over a five- or 10-year period, they will not only outperform any other asset class but will also help you keep pace with inflation when you retire.

Can you count on the Canada Pension Plan? I know there is a popular view that you shouldn't, but I don't agree. I believe Ottawa and the provinces do not have the political will to write it off. That much seems pretty clear now.

The CPP may be changed, though. In fact, it will probably undergo changes that include, at the very least, higher premiums and a higher retirement age. These changes are not likely to affect anyone who is about to retire in the next five years, but I believe they will certainly impact those in their 50s today.

Only three options for your RRSP money

If you turn 69 this year, you must collapse your RRSP and decide what to do with the proceeds before the end of the year. Basically, there are three options:

* **Cash out.** Simply collapse your RRSP and take out the proceeds in cash. The problem with this strategy is that the full amount is added to your taxable income and taxed at your full marginal rates. If you have $100,000 in your RRSP, for example, at least $50,000 will wind up in Revenue Canada's pockets.

* **Buy an annuity.** There are several options to choose from. You can buy an annuity which will pay you a guaranteed income for your life or until age 90. Given current interest rate levels, this is not your best option, either. Mind you, it could be — if rates suddenly rise to the 12%-to-15% level they were at a few years ago. This is not a likely scenario for some time.

* **Transfer your RRSP to a Registered Retirement Income Fund or RRIF.** At the moment, this is your best option. Basically, RRIFs are RRSPs in reverse. Instead of making a contribution every year, you'll be making withdrawals. How much? That depends on your age and your spouse's age.

Ottawa, in fact, has developed a formula which mandates the minimum income you must withdraw every year. Minimum withdrawal in your first year, for example, is 7.38%. The percentage goes up every year after that until you reach your 94th birthday, when the minimum withdrawal increases to 20% and stays at this level until your RRIF is exhausted.

There are no upper restrictions on how much you can take. As a rule, however, the more you take out and the earlier you do so, the shorter the time period you can count on support from your RRIF.

Many people don't really understand the purpose of RRIFs and how they work. In many ways, a RRIF is like a barrel of oil. If you puncture a hole in the bottom of the barrel, the oil will drip out slowly, and the hole may even get a bit bigger through use. Your RRIF is like that barrel. Once started, your money will continue to drip out, too.

You can never patch the barrel of oil — because oil is a lubricant, and no glue would stick — so the drip continues until the barrel is empty. The same with your RRIF. Once you start it, you can't stop it. If you need to make a lumpsum withdrawal on a one-time basis, perhaps to buy a new car or take the trip of a lifetime, you'd be far better off taking it out of your RRSP instead. Tapping your RRSP is like putting a pump on the top of the barrel and sucking out what you need. There's no hole on the bottom of the barrel — so you can lock it up after taking what you need, and nothing more comes out until you want it to.

I'm continuously amazed by the number of people who mistakenly start a RRIF before age 69, figuring this is the way to go, when they would be far better off to simply stay put and take out what they need at the time.

Another tip: If you decide to tap your RRSP, take the money out in small amounts — because the withholding taxes will be smaller. Come the end of the year, when you file your tax return, you'll settle up with whatever taxes you owe anyway, but in the meantime, at least, you won't have to pay any more taxes than necessary.

The big strength of RRIFs is their complete flexibility. In terms of investments, they are essentially bound by the same rules as RRSPs, including foreign content. In fact, you can transfer the investments you now hold inside your RRSP directly to your RRIF — without any changes — and adjust them at will to reflect your risk tolerance and the rate of return you will need for a comfortable retirement.

You can also have more than one RRIF — just as you can have more than one RRSP. Unlike individual RRSPs, however, which are relatively easy to administer and keep track of, RRIFs require considerably more attention because each one is required to make minimum payouts every year.

If you have more than one RRSP, your best strategy is to consolidate them into one or two RRIFs. This will not only simplify administration but make the management of their assets much easier as well.

Another key point. You don't need to be 69 to convert your RRSP to a RRIF. That's important if you plan to retire early, but there are a couple of caveats to keep in mind before you take that step. Once a RRIF is started, you can't change your mind later and stop it. Nor can you transfer your assets back to an RRSP, and you must start taking income out within a year — even if you have gone back to work in the meantime. Having to take out a minimum income stream each year can be a problem for many people, even in their early 70s, who have earned an investment income or even pension income outside their RRIFs.

This is where advance planning pays for itself in spades. Under current tax rules, you can delay taking RRIF income for years after the plan has been started. In addition, if your spouse is younger than you, Revenue Canada will allow you to use his or her age for the RRIF minimum income calculation. This little bit of planning can quite literally save you thousands of dollars.

Advance planning also comes into play if a sizeable chunk of your retirement portfolio is invested in GICs which come due a couple of years after you are required to start taking income from your RRSP. This can create enormous problems.

If you die, your RRIF assets will be taxed to the hilt. If you name your spouse as beneficiary, the assets can be transferred to your spouse tax-free. Your spouse can continue the RRIF or transfer the assets to his or her own RRSP if not yet 69 years of age.

Once your spouse dies — or even if there is no spouse — the entire proceeds of the RRIF are taken as income in the year of your death and taxed at your full marginal rate. If you're talking about $200,000 or $300,000, you know what that will amount to.

One solution is to take out insurance on your life and use the proceeds to pay off the taxes on your RRIF proceeds. A cheaper solution is to take out a joint insurance policy on your life and the life of your spouse to cover these taxes. The proceeds are payable on the death of the last-surviving spouse.

Beating the "Mac Gap"

In the U.S., they call it the "Mac Gap" — retirees who suddenly find they don't have enough money to live on and who are forced to take jobs at local fast-food restaurants to make up the difference. They aren't alone. Most of us vastly underestimate the amount of money we'll need to see us through our retirement years. There are basically only three solutions:

★ Change the way we invest.

★ Start investing early.

★ Reduce our living costs — now and in retirement.

Many people compound the problem by investing in the wrong vehicles — fixed-income investments like GICs — because they can't "take a chance" with their retirement money. Ironically, that's exactly what they're doing when they lock their retirement funds away in today's low-yielding GICs.

There is simply no possible way they can meet their targets by investing in low-rate securities that virtually guarantee they'll outlive their money. Study after study has shown there is only one asset class that has consistently outperformed all others — and that's equities. If there is a lesson, it's simply this: You have to invest in stocks early and stick with them for the rest of your life, whether you like the idea or not.

Even at age 65 — when most people become very conservative with their retirement funds — your money will have to work hard for you, in fact, for at least another 20 years. Unless stocks are part of your investment mix, there's a good chance you won't have enough money to see you through.

How much is enough? That depends on you, your time horizon, how much money you'll need to maintain your lifestyle, and, above all, how much the ups and downs of the stock market affect you emotionally.

Intellectually, most people understand that it is the nature of stocks to go up and down, that over a 10- or 20-year period, stocks will be significantly higher. Emotionally, it's quite another matter. Some people just can't handle the wild gyrations that convulse stock markets from time to time. Yet in order to ensure that their retirement income will be enough to meet their needs, this is something they will need to come to grips with.

When you start to save is just as important as what you invest in. Assuming an average compound rate of return of 10% a year, an individual who puts $2,000 a year in his RRSP, starting at age 21, will have $1,435,809.69 by the time he is ready to retire at age 65.

If that individual stops investing at age 35 — and just lets his savings grow until his 65th birthday — he will accumulate $1,073,922.76.

Compare these results with another individual who delays starting an RRSP until she reaches age 35 and puts aside $2,000 a year in a mutual fund that produces a 10% annual compound rate of return over the next 30 years.

At age 65, that person's savings will grow to $361,886.85 — not even remotely comparable to the nest egg built up by the person who starts at age 21 but infinitely better than failing to take action at all. To play catch-up, this individual would have to invest at least $7,900 in her RRSP every year from age 35 on.

Saving as much as we can during our working years is not easy given the level of financial obligations most of us face with young families, when our financial needs ironically are the greatest. Yet living within our means is critical if we hope to realize our dream of being able to retire early and without worry. Otherwise, we will surely run the risk of becoming another statistic in the growing "Mac Gap."

Even those who feel confident about their retirement are haunted by the spectre of outliving their money.

First off, even with the most generous corporate pension, your monthly income will drop by 35%. For many people who have become accustomed to a certain lifestyle, that can be a real shocker.

Take a minute and do a few calculations and you'll get a pretty good idea where you stand. That, of course, assumes you'll be able to retire on a company pension. If you are not so fortunate — and most Canadians are not — the problem is even more chilling.

In determining how much money you'll need to preserve your lifestyle, there are two other things to consider — the loss of the Old Age Pension as we know it today, and the impact of inflation on our purchasing power.

The average Canadian currently earns in the neighbourhood of $40,000. The clawback starts at $53,000. If the clawback starts at $50,000, for example, or lower, you should ask yourself what effect this will have on your pension. Will it be enough?

Inflation is low now — but that has not been the norm in the past, nor is it likely to be in the future. Using the historical average over the past three decades — you'll need $53,920 in just five years to match the spending power of $40,000 today. In 10 years, you'll need $59,210; in 15 years, $72,038; in 20 years, $87,645; and 25 years from now, you'll need $106,633 in income just to maintain a $40,000 standard of living.

This is important, particularly if your pension plan is not performing. If it isn't, you may want to supplement it with your own RRSP. Your company will provide this information for you.

It's also worth noting that some employees qualify for past-service pensions. If you're one of them, you can buy past service and fatten up for pension. Here your company will match your contribution, too. Talk to your financial planner about this and get solid advice before proceeding.

The RRSP contributions you make today are extremely important to the way you'll live in the future. You decide on the level of income you want and create an investment plan that will get you there. While it's important to make use of RRSPs as early as possible, it's never too late to start. Even in your late 60s, you'll save until you reach your 69th birthday, when your RRSP must be collapsed or invested in a RRIF.

RRIFs need growth, too

Many people think once they retire — or take out a RRIF — that their investment horizon just got a lot shorter. Not true. It's a common misconception and for many RRIF holders, who tend to think in these terms, a very costly one.

They forget that even if they're 70 years old, their savings must do them at least another 15 years — and, as a result, they fall into the trap of investing in things like GICs that are virtually guaranteed to erode their capital base.

Under current tax laws, you're required to withdraw an increasing amount from your RRIF every year. When you consider that you must take out 7.38% the first year and that a one-year GIC pays less than 6%, you get the picture very quickly about what will happen to your money at the end of 15 years.

The only way to make your money last longer is by putting a portion of your RRIF holdings into equities. The mix depends on you and your risk tolerance.

This is all the more important this year when a lot more people than usual will be taking out RRIFs — thanks to changes in the latest federal budget, which lowered the age when a RRSP must be turned into a RRIF from 71 to 69. If you're not sure what to do, or what you can live with in terms of market volatility, make sure you talk to a financial adviser. This year will be critical. And

204 Taking Care of *Your* Money

so will the investment strategy you ultimately adopt for your retirement funds.

RRIFs, by the way, cannot be transferred to your spouse on your death — if you're both over age 71. The surviving spouse must use the proceeds to take out an immediate annuity.

At the moment, many investors have their retirement money tied up in GICs and term deposits — and that's where their investment strategies will hit a major snag. Under current legislation, we must withdraw money at a predetermined schedule. At today's interest rates, that schedule will require GIC investors not only to remove all the interest they earn every year but to attack the principal as well. Unless interest rates rise — and rise substantially — and that's not likely over the foreseeable future, **there is a very real danger that this group will outlive their savings**.

Here's what I mean: If your RRIF has $100,000 invested in GICs, for example, it will earn 6.62% or $6,620 — yet you must withdraw a minimum of 7.38% or $7,380 in the first year. In the second year, the payout rate rises to 7.48%, and in the third year to 7.59%. By the sixth year, the rate jumps to 8%.

With a RRIF that's earning 6% a year, you'd be cutting into your principal by 1.5% a year. If this continues, it's only a question of time before you run out of money.

There's really only one solution — growth — and for most people, that translates into mutual funds, where the risk is spread over 30 or 40 stocks. For many of these investors, that won't be an easy decision, even though they understand the consequences of keeping their retirement savings in GICs or term deposits. That's essentially because mutual funds fluctuate on a daily basis — and that makes a lot of investors nervous. The problem is compounded if the mutual funds they've bought do not perform in the first or second year.

At some point, these investors will have to put a portion of their savings — or all of it — in equity-based mutual funds or be prepared to live on a lot less down the road. Once they come to that decision, the market will literally get a huge boost from hundreds of millions in new investment that wasn't there before.

That's one of the reasons segregated funds under a life insurance policy are becoming more and more popular. Segregated funds are identical to mutual funds but offer one distinct advantage — 100% of the principal of these funds is guaranteed upon death, no matter whether the stock market is up or down at the time.

This opens up a whole new avenue for individuals who need to create growth within their RRIF while creating a comfort zone for themselves.

Adding growth to your RRIF is important for two reasons:

* It will help you keep pace with RRIF payouts without dipping into your principal.

* It will increase the amount of money you'll be able to withdraw from your RRIF for the rest of your life.

Here's what happens when you invest $100,000 in a 6% GIC and a mutual fund with a compounded rate of return of 12% a year:

In the case of the 6% GIC, the $100,000 invested on June 1, 1996, for example, would grow to $103,517.81 by January 31, 1997 — the date when you start taking money out of your RRIF. First year's payout — $7,639.56. By the time you reach age 75, the value of the investment would drop to $94,425.75 and the payout to $7,544.52. By age 80, the $100,000 investment would shrink to $82,857.54 and the annual payout to $7,448.88. Five years later, when you reach 85, the value of the investment would decline to $67,962.86 and your annual stipend to $7,333.08.

The same $100,000 invested in a mutual fund averaging 12% a year would be worth $107,035.62 when you start withdrawing money from your RRIF at the rate of $7,899.12 a year. By age 75, the value of the investment would grow to $129,883.66 — despite the fact that the annual payout has risen to $10,377.60 — that's $2,833.08 more than a GIC-based RRIF would produce over the same period.

The gap grows even wider by the time you reach 80 and 85. By age 80, the investment would be worth $152,001.82 and the annual payout $13,664.88. By the time you reach age 85, the investment would grow to $166,633.36 (compared with $67,962.86 for the GIC) and the annual payout to $17,979.72 — more than double the $7,333.08 payout from the GIC-based RRIF.

Think about taking your CPP early

If you plan to retire prematurely, think about applying for the Canada Pension Plan when you do. As we know, Ottawa is reviewing the Canada Pension Plan, and there is no telling how this will turn out, given the huge unfunded liability bedevilling CPP planners.

So, whatever you get today may not be available a year or two from now. If you're 60, you'll qualify for a reduced pension — 70% of what you'll get at age 65. Payments are reduced by 0.5% a month (6% a year) when you apply for CPP before you reach your 65th birthday.

Each person's case is different — so have a financial planner assess the merits of taking or not taking CPP now. The planner will tell you how many years you have to keep working and contributing before it works against you, specifically the value of taking a reduced pension now. The break-even point — the point at which you actually start to lose by taking your CPP at age 60 — is 13 years — more if you invest the proceeds in a blue-chip equity fund until age 65.

If you're still not sure, ask yourself whether the Canada Pension Plan will stay as it is for the next 13 years. History suggests that when governments tinker with social benefits or programs like the Canada Pension Plan, the changes are not beneficial for the recipients.

Of course, if you wait until you're age 65 to collect, the monthly payment will be higher — but each month also represents a month in which you don't have the money. And that can add up to quite a tidy sum.

Also, if your eventual pension is going to be slightly higher for life — but clawed back — all you'll accomplish by waiting is to receive a bigger pension that will be clawed back. But if you get the cash now, the government can never take it from you later. That's worth remembering, too.

But delay starting a RRIF

It's pretty clear that Old Age Security benefits are next on Ottawa's hit list — and that could pose special problems for seniors who would like to withdraw money from their RRSPs and RRIFS.

The current clawback level is $53,215. Ottawa now wants to include all family income in that figure, and that could mean the end of these benefits for thousands of Canadians.

That's where effective tax-planning strategies come in.

First, delay starting a RRIF as long as possible. Once you do start, you can't stop. You must continue taking an income from the plan until all the funds inside it are exhausted. No matter what.

If you inherit some money later or sell your home and no longer need this money, you'll be stuck with taxable income you don't need — income that could put you over the $53,215 threshold.

Once you turn 69, you don't have a choice. By the end of the year in which you reach your 69th birthday — unless your spouse is younger and you can delay this process until he or she is 69 —

all the funds inside your RRSP must be transferred to a RRIF or to an annuity. Either that or your RRSP must be collapsed and taken into your income. In this instance, the funds will be taxed at your marginal rate.

If you want money to supplement your lifestyle, you're better off removing it from your RRSP. There will be a withholding tax on any amounts you withdraw — so keep withdrawals to less than $5,000 at a time to keep tax deductions to a minimum. Either way, you'll still face a bill for these withdrawals at tax time.

With an RRSP, you have complete flexibility. You don't have to take an income every year, and with Old Age Security benefits and the age 65 deduction on the table, that option can make all the difference.

Second, seek out the advice of an independent financial planner. He or she can help you withdraw some of those RRSP funds tax-free. Suppose, for example, you want to remove $5,000 a year for the next three years. One way is to buy $15,000 worth of mutual fund limited partnerships. You'll be required to put up $5,000 a year for three years — but you'll also receive a $5,000 tax deduction each year. This strategy will enable you to deduct $5,000 a year tax-free for three years — even though you don't actually get your hands on the money.

If you're not able to make use of the money, why bother? The main reason is that these partnerships are not only good investments in their own right but will also produce an income stream from your share of the fund company's management and redemption fees. Also, this money is now outside your RRSP and no longer subject to the same rules governing RRSP or RRIF withdrawals.

This strategy pays off nicely when you're forced to use a RRIF. In this scenario, all you need to do is buy mutual fund limited partnerships for the amount of money you're required to take from your RRIF each year. This will take some planning, though — because the tax deductions are spread over three years. A financial planner can help you develop a graduated purchase plan to meet your specific circumstances.

There are other types of limited partnerships such as film productions and computer programs that can provide even larger write-offs. Bear in mind that not all limited partnerships are created equal, and each should be judged on its investment merits.

RRIF better choice than annuity

While many Canadians remove money from their RRSPs via an annuity or by outright cancellation of their plans, there's a better choice — a Registered Retirement Income Fund or RRIF. It's better than an annuity because it offers more flexibility, lower tax rates, and the return of more of your money than you'd normally receive under an annuity.

At one time, we were allowed only one RRIF, which restricted us to a smaller monthly income than we could get from an annuity. That, of course, is now changed, and we can have as many RRIFs as we want.

With an annuity, we may never get all our money back — just a monthly income. With a RRIF, we get back all our original money plus all the investment income earned inside the plan.

And when it comes to comparing a RRIF to the third option — collapsing your RRSP outright and paying full tax on the proceeds — the RRIF comes out way ahead. With a RRIF, you spread the tax liability over 20 years or more. In fact, with proper planning, you can actually get most or all of the money out tax-free.

With an annuity, everything stops when you die — although many plans offer a 15-year guarantee. And if you live, you have to recognize that inflation will gradually destroy the purchasing power of your fixed-income annuity. In 15 years, that could be quite substantial.

With a RRIF, you'll be able to increase your monthly income every five years — and still have a healthy balance left in the plan after 15 years. It will continue to produce an income for your life and the life of your spouse. And enable you to leave a sizeable amount for your heirs should you both pass away.

Make your home part
of your retirement plan

Your home should be an integral part of your retirement plan. That's right. Your home. We sometimes forget that our homes are one of the few tax-free investments left to us — and hence a great way to accumulate money for our retirement.

While all other investments produce taxable income, your principal residence is allowed to compound completely free of tax. In fact, you can even upgrade on a regular basis to a more expensive principal residence — it must be your principal residence — and all existing and future gains will be tax-free.

If you buy investments that rise in value, they do so tax-free until they are sold. Even then, one-quarter of the capital gain will escape taxation. The balance, or three-quarters, of the gain must be added to your income and taxed at your normal rate. In addition, any interest or dividend income produced by the investment is taxed in the year it is earned.

RRSPs are a different story. They provide a tax deduction when you put the money in as well as tax-free compounding for as long as the money remains inside the plan.

Both your RRSP and your principal residence grow tax-free — but the RRSP will produce taxable income when you withdraw money. This is not an option once you transfer assets to a RRIF. Under current rules, you must begin to withdraw funds no later than a year after you establish the RRIF. In some cases, the amount could be enough to push you over the clawback level and reduce any social benefits you would ordinarily be entitled to.

Given this scenario, you would assume that a house is a better deal than an RRSP. Not necessarily so. Both play a role in any meaningful financial plan. In today's high-tax environment, it pays to take every deduction you can possibly get. And given today's low-interest rate levels, it also pays to borrow as much as you can to own the most valuable principal residence possible.

Where does this leave other investments, like mutual funds and stocks? I believe they should play a major role in every investment/retirement strategy. In fact, your house fits into this strategy very neatly. Once you've been able to amass enough money for the down payment, you will have a forced savings plan. You must make monthly payments, or you lose your house.

Forced savings plans have proven to be the most successful way to save for the average investor. The odds are that if you take the money home, you'll spend it. If it disappears before you get a chance to spend it, you'll have it for future use.

We can use the same strategy when it comes to buying other investments, like stocks and mutual funds. You should compare the benefits of making higher or extra payments on your mortgage or using these funds to acquire other investments. Each has a value, but a combination of the two will ultimately produce the best results, as far as most people are concerned.

As a rule, you should always contribute to your RRSP when you have extra money. You'll not only save taxes but also enjoy tax-free compounding. You should then accumulate money to pay against your mortgage. However, any time you pay down your mortgage, think about borrowing an equal amount to buy investments.

We know that, given a reasonable period of time, good-quality mutual funds will outperform real estate. In addition, you'll get some tax relief while you're waiting. If you pay $5,000, for example, against your mortgage and then reborrow to buy investments, the interest on the new loan is tax deductible.

Bottom line: You then own a house that rises in value tax-free, plus a tax deduction because of the interest cost on the borrowed funds, as well as investments that also rise in value — a great multi-dimensional strategy that will pay off big-time at retirement.

Funeral planning: Make it part of your retirement plan

Thinking about preplanning your funeral? A lot of people are. In fact, many even pay for everything in advance — right down to the newspaper notices. Big advantage — you're doing it at a time when you and your spouse are in a rational state of mind. That's important, because you'll be making decisions about the kind of funeral you want — not what your children or relatives think you should have.

The average cost of a funeral today is about $5,000, plus another $1,000 to $1,500 for extra services provided by the funeral home on your instructions. These include death and regulatory fees, the cost of opening and closing the grave, church/clergy fees, newspaper notices, flowers, even GST.

If you prepay these costs, you'll be paying for a service you will use tomorrow in today's dollars. Here's how it works: After you decide on all these things, including the kind of casket you would like and the type of religious service, you write a cheque to the funeral home for the total — for example, $6,500.

The funeral home prepays all items it is able to in advance, such as cemetery or cremation charges. The cemetery/crematorium issues a certificate to the funeral home indicating that these services have been paid for and will be rendered when required. The balance of the funds is placed in a third-party trust in your name, not in the name of the funeral home. These funds are not dispersed to the funeral home until the trust is satisfied that you have died and funeral arrangements have been carried out.

One key caveat: Find out what guarantee the funeral home offers on the prepaid funds. Not all funeral homes offer the same guarantee. Here's what to look for: If the trust fund, with accumulated interest, has more money in it than the funeral home's costs at the time of the funeral, the surplus is returned to your estate. If the fund does not have enough money in it to meet these costs at the time of your death, the shortfall is assumed by the funeral home. As long as you do not change these arrangements, the funeral home will guarantee that the funds on deposit, plus accumulated interest, will provide these services when required.

In Ontario, for example, the funeral home places your money with an institution called Guaranteed Funeral Deposits of Ontario, which was set up to administer funds for funeral homes. Under this arrangement, the funeral home must invest this money to generate a level of interest at least equal to the interest paid on Canada Savings Bonds in any given year.

Funeral service costs, like any other service, are subject to inflation. As a rule, the increase in funeral costs is somewhat less than the annual rate of inflation. Cemetery costs are normally based on the cost of replacing the plot sold to you at the time. In that sense, cemeteries are like any other piece of real estate — the closer they are to downtown, the more the plots will cost.

A note of caution: Make sure you discuss your plans with your family before preplanning your funeral — in particular, what you plan to do and why you want to do it. If no one in your family has ever been cremated, and this is what you plan to do, it can be quite a shock to your family if they don't know in advance. Always keep in mind that your funeral is not for you but for your family and friends. (Cremation, by the way, has become quite popular in recent years. In Toronto, about half of all funerals end in cremation, and the trend is accelerating.)

A final note on costs: The Canada Pension Plan has a death benefit that can be used to pay for the cost of your funeral, amounting to a $3,500 lump sum payment for someone who has never taken benefits. For someone who has, the benefit amounts to five times his or her monthly CPP cheque.

Is prepaying a good idea? It depends — on your age, life expectancy, the rate of inflation, what you can earn on an alternative investment, and the risks involved in that investment.

If you prepay $5,000, for example, and die nine years later, your $5,000 would be worth $9,192 — assuming an annual compound rate of return of 7%. If you invest the $5,000 in a mutual fund that averages 10.5% a year over the same period — many dividend funds do that — your $5,000 would now be worth $12,280.

If, during the same period, inflation averages 3% a year, the cost of an average funeral — currently about $5,000 — would rise to $6,524.

Either way, you're ahead — in the case of prepayment by $3,388, and by $5,766 with the mutual fund.

When it comes to money, however, timing is everything. If you bought an equity fund, for example, and the market promptly went into a nosedive, resulting in a 10% loss, and you had the misfortune to die during that period, your estate would be out $515 (capital loss and inflation).

Chapter 9

Taxing Times

The Romans imposed a tax on dying.
Did failure to pay the tax mean
that you couldn't die? Absolutely not.
It meant that the dead couldn't be buried.

Always think tax first

If you're like thousands of Canadians who wait to the last minute every year to file their tax returns, you're in good company. And in smart company, too, if you owe Revenue Canada money. In fact, that's exactly how you should plan it every year.

I know many people prefer to have the government owe them because they have a hard time coming up with the cash at tax time. From a financial-planning point of view, that's little more than a forced savings program — and a poor one at that. You'd be far better off paying the correct amount — or ideally, a bit less — and using the difference to invest in a good blue-chip equity fund throughout the year.

I can tell you that you'll be much further ahead in 10 years' time — no matter what the fund earns — than making sure you don't owe Revenue Canada at tax time.

Make it a point, in fact, to consider the tax consequences of every financial move you make. This can range from something as complicated as estate planning to something as simple as switching out of one mutual fund and into another. If there is a capital gain involved, you will have to pay a tax on that gain — even if both funds belong to the same family. What counts, as far as Revenue Canada is concerned, is whether the investments are outside your RRSP. Keep that in mind next time you think about switching funds.

When it comes to tax planning, here are a few more things to consider:

Capital disposition planning. Timing, as they say, is everything. That includes when you dispose of your investments. To utilize this strategy to the fullest, make it a point to review your tax position and investment portfolio every year, ideally before the end of November. In fact, it's a good time to review all your investments with timing in mind. Has the investment matured? Is it in a sector that's facing tough times?

This will help you identify those investments that have accrued capital gains or losses and determine whether it's to your advantage to sell any of them, especially the losers. We all have them.

If you lock in the loss before the end of the year, you'll be able to use the loss to offset gains on other investments you may have. Take note, however, that this must be done on or before the TSE's last trading date for settlement. That's always before the end of the year.

If your spouse owns a few clunkers but can't use the capital loss, consider purchasing the investments from your spouse at fair market price. This will enable you to claim the accrued capital loss when you sell the security later to someone else.

Key point: If you sell a stock or mutual fund for the loss, neither you nor your spouse may buy it back within 30 days. If you do, the loss will be disallowed for tax purposes.

Tax shelters. A great way to reduce taxes — but always keep in mind that not all tax shelters are alike. Each should be judged first of all on its investment merits, not on its ability to generate tax relief. Spending $1 to get 50 cents' worth of tax relief is hardly a good trade-off.

Also keep in mind that Revenue Canada has a policy of reassessing tax shelters, specifically as to whether they were developed solely to provide tax relief. Tax shelters that offer no prospect of earning a profit are usually disallowed. Another reason to make sure that the investment stands up on its own.

Tax shelters worth considering include flow-through shares, oil and gas limited partnerships, as well as shelters that invest in real estate, providing — and this is a key point — that the underlying real estate investment is whole and not just another investment vehicle designed solely to manufacture tax relief.

A number of overvalued real estate tax shelters, where the underlying value did not meet Revenue Canada's standards, made it virtually impossible for the investor to catch up. Even if Revenue Canada *had* allowed them to stay on the books, the investments would never have caught up.

Mutual fund and software limited partnerships, also great favourites, are now gone. That's why it's more important than ever to develop and put in place proper tax planning.

When it comes to tax shelters, always consider the impact the shelter may have on the Alternative Minimum Tax or AMT. If you have a minimum tax liability and have used forward averaging before 1988, think about bringing the forward-averaged amounts into income to reduce AMT. Also take note that, beginning in 1997, the $40,000 AMT threshold is reduced to $25,000.

Pension-income credit. If you are not fully utilizing your pension-income credit, think about buying an annuity or a RRIF which will provide annual pension income.

Alimony and maintenance. Under proposals made in the 1996 federal budget, child support and spousal support will be treated differently. Spousal support will continue to be treated as in the past for tax purposes, but there will be a change to the way child-support agreements or court orders made after April 30, 1997, are taxed. After that date, child-support payments will no longer be deductible for the payer nor included in the income of the spouse receiving the payments.

RRSP designation. Most individuals designate their spouses as beneficiaries of their RRSPs — for good reason. Under existing tax rules, RRSPs can pass directly to a surviving spouse's RRSP or RRIF untaxed. Designating your spouse in your will is not enough. He or she must also be designated as your beneficiary under your RRSP. Otherwise, at least 50% of the value of your RRSP holdings will find its way into the tax collector's hands when you die.

There's hidden gold in old tax returns

What you learn from last year's tax return could make a big difference in your after-tax income for years to come. It's worth the time. Thousands of Canadians have already benefited from the exercise — and so should you.

That's one of the big advantages of using a software program like *Brian Costello's HomeTax*, which has a special diagnostic feature that enables you to go through a series of "what if" scenarios and determine what effect each alternative would have on your tax return.

Often this exercise will turn up tax-cutting opportunities that you might otherwise have missed or that you deliberately omitted because you did not understand these deductions would have been allowed by Revenue Canada.

I've received dozens of letters from people all over Canada who got back thousands of dollars in tax rebates because of missed opportunities going back a number of years. Many taxpayers, in fact, don't realize they have the option of reopening past tax returns to claim unused tax deductions in previous years — missed medical deductions or, for example, failing to use carry-forward or carry-back options to their advantage.

Failure to declare losses on rental properties is a classic example. Many people who, for example, earned $14,000 in rental income and had $16,000 in legitimate expenses fail to claim the $2,000 loss. For many, it's simply a case of not knowing they have this option. It's a very common misconception. And a costly one. That loss, even one as small as $2,000, is important because it comes off your taxable income. For an individual in a 50% tax bracket, that loss is worth $1,000 in tax savings — and not just for 1995.

Under current tax laws, you can reopen previous tax returns as far back as 1987, so that $2,000 you failed to declare in 1995 may really be worth $16,000 — or a tax rebate of about $8,000.

The rationale behind this is that Ottawa is going to share in any profits your property will earn down the road. It will certainly share in any capital gains resulting from the sale of the property. So use your partner today — and make sure it pays its fair share. It'll get its tomorrow. Count on it.

Pay special attention, too, to the interest-income line on your return. If you earn interest from fixed-income investments, you already know you're not getting any tax breaks. Think about switching to preferred or common shares that pay dividends instead. As a rule of thumb, every dollar in dividend income produces the same after-tax returns as $1.25 in interest income. That's because dividends qualify for a special tax break called the dividend tax credit.

Here's how it works — and why it's a little confusing. If you receive $100 in dividends, for example, you must declare $125 on your tax return. In another area of your return, you get a dividend tax credit of 13.33%. Remember, this is a tax credit — not a deduction from taxable income. That's why it works in your favour.

There is, however, another, perhaps more compelling, reason for switching to dividend-paying stocks or, better still, a dividend fund. Fixed-income investments like GICs have been producing less and less income since 1981, when interest rates peaked. During the same time, the amount of dividends paid by Canadian corporations has actually been going up — and will probably continue to grow as the economy improves.

Bottom line: With dividends, you'll wind up earning more. And keeping more.

Know the rules — or someone who does

The story is different, but the twist is the same. So is the result, which is most often painful and very costly for the individual. In most cases, it's because the individual gets lost in the complex world of financial planning and makes mistakes he or she wishes to forget.

Here's a classic that happens hundreds of times a year across Canada. An individual has a mortgage coming up for renewal. He also has enough money inside his RRSP to pay off the mortgage and, understandably, decides to cash in the RRSP and do just that. On the surface, this strategy looks reasonable, but in actual fact it usually turns out to be a tragic mistake.

It makes a great deal of sense to save taxes, especially when it's a simple matter of paying off a loan that is not tax deductible. In some cases, it's more obvious than in others. In this instance, the individual had his RRSP at the same institution where he had his mortgage. The lending institution wanted to charge a higher rate on the mortgage when it came up for renewal than it paid on the term deposits inside his RRSP.

This individual had a hard time understanding this because the amount of money involved was virtually the same. For him, it just made sense to cash in his RRSP, pay off the mortgage, and save all the interest he was paying on the mortgage. He figured he could then take the payments he was making on his mortgage and rebuild his RRSP.

Unfortunately, he forgot all about the tax collector. When you remove money from your RRSP, it must be added to your income and taxed at your highest marginal tax rate. The institution told him there would be a withholding tax when the money was removed, but he didn't realize that this was not all and that the balance had to be paid when he filed his return.

The withholding tax starts at 10% on amounts less than $5,000 and rises to a high of 30% on amounts over $15,000. If your tax rate is low, you might well pay back less than you saved in taxes. However, if you're like this individual, the tax surprise may be so great that it's better to keep the money inside your RRSP. This individual was in the 40% tax bracket. That meant he would eventually pay approximately 40% tax on all the funds he removed from his RRSP. Paying a 40% penalty to get your hands on RRSP money to pay off your mortgage is just a little too rich in my books.

His problem didn't end there. He used all the cash from his RRSP to pay off his mortgage. Because the withholding tax didn't comprise his entire tax bill, he now had to save up extra money throughout the rest of the year to pay his tax bill rather than start recontributing to his RRSP. In addition, his penalty was actually higher than 40% when you factor in the 6% the term deposits were earning inside his RRSP. The advantage, of course, was that he got to eliminate his mortgage and save about 14% to 16% a year in pre-tax dollars.

There is a way around this pain for some. If you qualify to contribute to an RRSP, you can look at putting some money back in. How much depends on your contribution limit and if you have any unused contribution room. There are a few other choices. In this case, he could have opened a self-directed RRSP and had his RRSP lend him the money to pay off the mortgage. There would have been no tax consequences — as he would only have borrowed the money, not removed it, from his RRSP. A neat but important distinction that would literally have saved him thousands of dollars.

The lesson is a simple one. Know the rules — or someone who does — before you burn bridges you may later need to cross.

What to do with your tax rebate

First of all, you should try your best not to get a tax rebate. This isn't a gift. It's a return of your own money that was mistakenly held from your paycheque by Revenue Canada. And all the time it's had use of your money, it hasn't had to pay one cent of interest — interest you could have earned if you had put this money in an investment.

If you receive a nice fat tax-rebate cheque every year, you should take a few minutes to reassess your situation and what you can do about it.

You can either ask your employer to reduce your withholding taxes or, if you need a forced savings plan (some people use withholding taxes as a form of forced savings plan), have an amount equal to the tax overpayment deducted from your pay and used to buy Canada Savings Bonds on the Payroll Savings Plan. Another option would be to buy mutual funds on automatic monthly payment plans or anything else that will produce a chunk of money each spring — money that has also been earning interest as it was accumulating.

But that's for next year. What should we do with this year's tax rebate?

My first choice is to try to multiply its value. The easiest way — before you're tempted to do something else with it — is to contribute it to your RRSP. Use it to produce even more money. Before doing this, you'll have to determine whether there is room in your tax situation for an RRSP contribution. If there isn't, perhaps you might consider making an additional contribution to your company's pension plan.

However, if you can make a contribution to your RRSP, you'll be a double winner. You manufacture an instant tax deduction, and you can save taxes on any investment income you earn. You can also ask your employer to treat this contribution as an immediate tax deduction. This will increase your take-home pay and give you more disposable income throughout the year.

The second way you win is by saving taxes on investment income earned inside your RRSP.

If you don't want to — or cannot — contribute to your RRSP, you have a variety of other choices. You can spend it or use it to pay down your mortgage, your credit card bills, or even your car loan.

Whatever you do, it always pays to adopt a multi-dimensional strategy. For example, if you pay down your mortgage, think about borrowing an equal amount to buy investments. The interest on the new loan is now tax deductible — and this, in turn, will manufacture further tax savings. In addition, the investment should pay off handsomely down the road.

By using this strategy, your entire mortgage will be tax deductible eventually, effectively cutting your interest costs in half.

Depending on the size of your rebate, give some thought to using the money to acquire investments that will produce tax rebates next year. It may be enough to get you started in an oil and gas fund, a Registered Education Savings Plan, or even a mutual fund limited partnership.

Dividend reinvestment programs:
Commission-free investing

If you usually deposit your dividend cheques in a savings account when you receive them, think about reinvesting the proceeds in additional shares of the company. A number of companies offer this option and enable you to reinvest this money, no matter how small the amount, in more shares — with no sales commissions or charges of any kind.

This is an important point because many people feel that, because the amount of money involved is so small, they might as well just let it sit in their savings accounts. A far smarter move would be to reinvest this money in more of that company's shares rather than let it gather dust in your account. Not only are today's interest rates low, but taxes must also be paid on any interest earned on this money.

Dividend reinvestment programs are a win-win deal all the way around — you'll be able to acquire more shares commission-free and in some cases at 5% to 10% below the going market price. The company will love it because it will be able to issue new shares instead of paying money out as dividends. That's a lot cheaper than borrowing money or going to the expense of an under-writing. You won't escape taxes — even though you don't actually see the cash — but the income will be tax-advantaged.

There's another advantage that often gets overlooked. The most successful investors are often those who make good use of a systematic investment program, in which they invest a certain amount every month or every quarter on a planned, systematic basis — no matter what is happening in the stock market at the time. History shows that high-quality stocks generally rise over time, and their shareholders, more often than not, wind up with a substantial windfall down the road. Many large companies pay dividends quarterly — a natural fit for any systematic investment program that can work wonders for your retirement.

Dividend reinvestment programs have been one of the marvellous advantages of owning mutual funds. Under this program, unitholders have the option of reinvesting all dividends declared by the fund into more shares of that fund.

There are two types of distributions: dividends paid on capital gains earned by the fund, and interest income earned on the fund's assets during the year. If these dividends are paid on shares of mutual funds you hold outside your RRSP, they are taxable — even though you do not receive them in cash — and must be reported to Revenue Canada when you file your tax return. As such, they will qualify for the dividend tax credit. If earned by a fund with a high foreign content, they may qualify for the foreign tax credit. Whatever the case, make sure you ask your fund company or financial planner whether you are entitled to the foreign tax credit.

Most funds also earn interest on their investments — and they will report this interest to you. This should be sent to you on a T5 slip at tax time, but if it is not, it is your obligation to obtain this information and declare the income on your tax return.

How you take the dividend is up to you. If you don't need the income, your best bet is to reinvest the dividends in more shares. Before too long, you'll be earning shares on the shares you earned as dividends and really taking advantage of the magic of compounding.

Benefits vs. salary

There's a lot to be said for tax-free benefits. In fact, there's a lot to be said for benefits, even if they are taxable. Beware, though, as governments are looking at more ways to tax benefits. The last federal budget, for example, changed a long-standing benefit enjoyed by millions of employees — company-paid premiums on employee insurance policies up to $25,000. Those premiums must now be treated as taxable benefits — even though you don't actually get the cash.

There are many benefits that are still tax-free, though. If you are planning to buy a similar benefit for yourself, for example, you could probably get it cheaper through your employer than you could buying it on your own.

I find, however, that too many employees don't want benefits. They prefer a fatter paycheque, even though they have to pay tax on that income and have much less purchasing power after the tax collector has reaped the government's share.

A classic example is an employer-sponsored pension or deferred profit-sharing plan. If you contribute to an RRSP or a registered pension plan, you get a tax deduction for the amount you contribute. However, if your employer matches the amount you contribute to an employer-sponsored plan, you get double the bang for your buck — but with no taxable benefit.

Many employees make the mistake of calculating whether they should contribute to a pension plan or an RRSP during the RRSP season. But that's too late. While we get an extra 60 days after the year-end to contribute to an RRSP, all contributions to a registered pension plan must be in the plan before the year ends.

With employers granting only small increases, many employees are using this route to get some extra cash out of their companies and, at the same time, some tax relief. They get a tax deduction for their contribution plus some free tax money out of their company.

One word of caution: It sounds nice to double your money in the first year, but many RRSPs outperform pension plans in the long run. So it pays to look at the past performance record of your company pension plan and see how it compares with the performance of one of the mutual funds inside your RRSP. A second consideration has to do with vesting requirements attached to your pension. If you aren't going to stay with the company for a long time, you may not want to put any money into the company pension plan at all. In that case, you should opt totally for an RRSP.

Many companies will pay tuition fees for courses. If the course is for the employer's benefit, you should not incur a taxable benefit. Likewise, if you are obliged to wear a distinctive uniform or special clothing like safety shoes and glasses, it would be better to get your employer to pay for them as you will not incur a taxable benefit.

Employers are allowed to reimburse us tax-free for reasonable out-of-pocket expenses when we're on business. That can include worldwide travel or gas and parking when we're out running errands for our employers.

If your company transfers you to another city, it can pick up your travel expenses without creating a tax liability for you. If you take a loss when you sell your house, the company can also reimburse you for that loss tax-free.

The same applies to the cost of joining a golf club. Employers are also allowed to give us a variety of other useful perks, such as employee discounts. Your company can also subsidize meals, provided the employee pays a reasonable charge, as well as employee counselling for self-improvement, stress relief, sales tools, job retraining, job placement, even legal and financial planning.

Bottom line: It pays to know what's taxable and what's not. A new health care package, for example, may put more dollars in your pocket at tax time than a shiny, new company car. So, if you have the option of renegotiating your compensation package or negotiating one at a new job, you'll be further ahead opting for benefits that don't carry a tax price tag.

Cars pose the most problem. Much depends on how you're reimbursed for the use of your car and whether you drive a company car. If you are reimbursed for the use of your car on company business, this money also escapes the tax collector's net.

When it comes to the use of your car, however, the key is what Revenue Canada considers a reasonable per-kilometre allowance, which may be more or less than what your company pays.

On the other hand, if you receive a monthly allowance from your employer for the use of your car — without reference to the distance travelled — this allowance must be included in your income. In this case, you may be able to deduct certain auto expenses to offset this income. The same rule applies if you use your car on company business and are not reimbursed for it.

In order to deduct these expenses — or at least a portion of them — there are a few bookkeeping chores. You must keep a record of all expenses and make sure you retain the receipts. You must also keep a record of distance travelled for business and complete Form T2200 or Declaration of Conditions of Employment Form.

If you are given a company car to use by your employer, the car is also considered a taxable benefit. This benefit, called a standby charge in accounting terms, is 2% of the original cost of the auto per month. This can be reduced if at least 90% of the distance travelled is for business, while personal use is fewer than 12,000 kilometres a year. If the car is leased by the company on your behalf, the benefit is two-thirds of the lease cost, excluding the cost of insurance.

If your company pays for any operating costs that relate to your personal use of the company car, this amount is also considered a taxable benefit and will be added to your income. This benefit is calculated at 13 cents times the number of personal kilometres driven in a year — less any amounts repaid to your employer for this use within 45 days after the end of the year.

If you want to cut the standby charge to 50%, the vehicle must be used at least 50% for business. If business use is less than 50%, consider paying for the personal portion of the operating costs yourself. After you've done all this, decide whether it's more advantageous for you or for your employer to own or lease the car.

Delay accepting income whenever possible

While we all want to earn as much as possible, there are times when we should consider refusing, or at least delaying, receipt of it.

Here's a classic example. It's late in the year and you're waiting for your annual bonus cheque. Welcome or not, it may be more profitable for you to ask your boss to delay giving it to you until the new year. While you won't have access to it for a couple of weeks or a few days, you also won't have to claim it as taxable income until next year. That means you won't have to settle up with the tax collector for at least another 14 months. It also means that being able to invest the tax share on this money for an extra 14 months will normally more than offset the loss of the bonus for a few days.

When we work for an employer, he or she will normally withhold taxes from our earnings. As long as the taxes are withheld on 70% of our earnings, we don't have to pay quarterly instalments on other income. We'll sort that out when we file our tax return.

If you have other forms of income, this planning can also pay dividends in another way. If you delay your bonus income until next year, you may now be able to defer paying quarterly instalments on freelance income. Conversely, if you have not kept up to quarterly instalments for the year, taking the bonus this year rather than next could save you having to pay some interest to Revenue Canada.

There are other instances in which this strategy will work just as effectively. That's where the advice of your financial planner can make all the difference.

Don't forget about CNIL-ity

Tie a string around your finger if you have to. But don't forget about CNIL-ity. If you do, you could bump your head on a potentially painful tax problem that could cost you thousands of dollars over a lifetime.

Many investors were able to enjoy "double dipping" — borrowing for investment purposes and using the proceeds to buy tax shelters like flow-through shares that produce a tax deduction. In these instances, investors were often able to claim the interest as an investment expense or as a tax deduction against other forms of income. The same for tax shelters. With the result that many investors purposely chose investments that did not produce much of a yield. This strategy, in effect, enabled them to save even more taxes on their other income.

Ottawa didn't take long to catch on to this strategy and quickly moved to plug the hole. The result — the Cumulative Net Investment Loss rule or CNIL, for short. This rule states that when you create an investment deduction by borrowing to buy investments, tax shelters, or other similar investments and claim this loss against income, you must claim an equivalent amount of taxable capital gains.

Suppose I had an interest expense of $1,000 and applied that expense against my salary income. I would have to offset this by reducing any capital gains realized that year by a similar amount — as though the gains were fully taxable.

CNIL still works — notwithstanding these changes. It's still valuable because it gives you long-term compounding. What you do is take the tax deduction now and perhaps recapture down the road when tax rates are lower. Remember that only 75% of the capital gain is taxable — so you actually wind up with a 100% tax deduction, but you only pay back 75 cents on the dollar. That's why it always pays to calculate and think CNIL whenever you manufacture investment expenses.

A new way to protect your RRSP assets from the tax collector

Budget changes to charitable donation limits have added a new wrinkle to tax and estate planning.

Until 1995, the ceiling on allowable charitable contributions for tax purposes was 20% of our taxable income. In 1996, this limit was increased to 50%, and to 75% in the 1997 budget.

In the year of your death, you can give away 100% — and therein lies a significant tax-saving strategy that benefits everyone except the tax collector.

Under existing rules, you can transfer your RRSPs to your spouse tax-free when you die. But when your spouse dies, these RRSPs are taxed at his or her marginal rate, effectively cutting the value of the RRSP assets in half. If you're single, it's pretty simple. You die, and the government gets to keep half. In either case, you should sit down with a financial planner and do an assessment of what your estate would look like at your death.

That's not as difficult as it sounds. There are life-expectancy tables that will give you a ballpark idea of how long you can expect to live.

The next step is to make a realistic assessment of your risk comfort level. This, in turn, will give you and your financial planner a pretty good idea of what to expect in the way of returns in the years you have left to retirement and how much your RRSP portfolio would likely be worth at that time.

If it works out to $500,000, for example, half of that money, or $250,000, will go to the tax collector when you and your spouse die.

Here's where the new wrinkle comes in: Take out a life insurance policy on your life, and do it today — the cheapest you can buy. Then donate the proceeds of the insurance to a charity of your choice at the same time.

This strategy will instantly trigger a tax deduction when you die — $500,000 in this example. The $500,000 contribution to the charity will, in effect, wipe out all the income represented by your RRSPs at that time and, in the process, all the taxes that might otherwise be levied on your RRSP holdings. As noted earlier, it's a win-win situation for everyone except Revenue Canada.

What about the cost of premiums? Much, much cheaper than a $250,000 tax bill for your heirs.

A final note: If you have a spouse, think in terms of a joint and last-survivor policy. It's cheaper still.

Chapter 10

Lessons Learned

Money is like a sixth sense —
you can't use the other five without it.

Longevity is pretty important when it comes to handling your money. In fact, I'd say it's critical. That even applies to telling people what to do with their money. I've lasted 27 years primarily, I believe, because I think rationally and follow some very specific rules — not just what I learned along the way but also from others with a lot more savvy and longevity than I have in the field. Here are some of the most important rules that have helped me to achieve the investment success I've enjoyed:

Even if you're on the right track, you'll get run over if you just sit there. That's because times change. And to succeed, you have to change with them. This is a paraphrase of a remark made by Mark Twain and quoted earlier in this book. His comment was not directed to investors or investments, but it works here, too,

234 Taking Care of *Your* Money

and pretty well sums up the approach we should adopt as investors.

You don't need risk. There is no need to take on undue risk to achieve your financial goals. There's a risk to just about any investment, even as something as safe as Canada Savings Bonds. Admittedly, not much. But still some. Theoretically, the government could go broke. New York did — although that's not a likely scenario in our case. The bottom line is that there's always a bit of risk to every investment. What we, as investors, must do is go through the whole risk spectrum and ask ourselves what degree of risk we're prepared to live with. As a rule, the greater the degree of risk, the greater rate of return we can expect. But why take on risk? Why not just buy quality investments? In the real estate industry, they talk about *location, location, and location.* In financial planning, you should think and talk *quality, quality, and quality.* As a rule, too, the greater the degree of quality, the less risk you take on. You must, however, take on some risk if you want to get a better rate of return. The challenge for us, as investors, is how to eliminate the risk and still get the yield that normally goes with that level of risk.

Generally, that's through diversification. Diversification is a key component to a carefully crafted multi-dimensional investment strategy — basically putting in place investments and strategies that overlap so that the risk is either diminished or eliminated. If you make investments that fluctuate, you lose — perhaps a lot — if they suddenly drop one day the way Bre-X did, with no hope of ever going back up. But if you have investments that go up and down but offer a regular yield, you can afford to wait until your investments go back up, because that yield will continue, no matter what happens in the meantime.

It's the same if you go out and buy a piece of raw land. If the price drops after you buy it, you may have to wait quite a long time before you can get your money back. Even then, you have to get a lot more than you paid because you lost the use of that money, which would have produced an income or profit if invested elsewhere during the interval. However, if I turn that land into a farm or a parking lot, I'll have some income while I'm waiting out the lulls in the market. As we can see, quality, like diversification, is extremely important to the process.

Always think taxes first. If you think yield first, then the yield will be taxable. In Canada, we pay taxes at every level. When we go to work, up to half of our income goes to the government. If we have a bit left over after that and invest it, we'll also be taxed on any profits or income generated by that investment. And then, when we die, Revenue Canada will also tax our estate. Or at least a part of it. In effect, we'll wind up getting taxed three times on essentially the same money along the way.

You have to think taxes first because you'll earn more by saving taxes than by investing the money. That's why you should make it a rule to take every tax deduction you can find and defer taxes for as long as you possibly can. That way you'll have the use of that money, which in turn can be used to produce even more income for you and your retirement fund. **Bottom line:** Do not pay one penny more tax than necessary — unless you think the government is going to support you in your old age. We've been finding out that there's less and less chance of that happening as we head into the new millennium.

That brings me to another cardinal rule: **Do not count on anyone else to do it for you. You must learn to depend on yourself. You have to put yourself in a position where you can control your own destiny.** Your RRSP is a classic example on the positive side. Here's one on the negative side: If you put your money in a deposit-taking institution like a bank, you're effectively lending your money to it, and in turn it will lend your money to someone else. It could be to a Third World country or to finance an oil tanker which could sink — or some other risky investment over which you have no control or say. That's why a self-directed RRSP is important. It does give you control over where your money is invested. It's your money, and you should have some say. By that I mean complete say.

Always use a pro. When we watch professional sports, be it golf, football, or hockey, we see the best there is. You want the best in the financial field quarterbacking your money for you. When you do it yourself, you essentially have a part-time financial planner working for you. Your money is too important to you to handle it on a part-time basis.

Don't be chintzy on the cost. People often tell me a financial planner costs too much money. Ideally, a financial planner should not cost you any money at all. In fact, a good financial planner will save you more in taxes than his or her fees could possibly cost.

Always use someone who has no bias. You need independent advice because you need to know at all times you're getting the straight goods. In everything. Someone who has an understanding of taxes, investments, life insurance, income splitting, etc. Above all, someone who is not a sales person in the classic sense of the word.

Forget the rearview mirror. It's great if you're driving but not when it comes to investing. Look forward. Not backward. If you look backward, your thinking will be shaped by what happened in the past, including performance and extrapolating that to the future. Unfortunately, that's not the way it is in the real world. You must be proactive and look ahead to what is going to happen so that you'll be able to protect yourself or position yourself to take advantage of any unforeseen opportunities that may arise.

Do not even dream of trying to time the market. When it comes to stock markets, it's always time. Not timing. Time always works in your favour providing you have put yourself in the right position, or against you if you haven't positioned yourself accordingly.

Classic example: A term deposit, which earns 4% a year, of which 2% is lost in taxes and the other 2% to inflation. If you think you've managed to break even, think again. The 2% inflation rate recorded in 1997 will not repeat itself next year, even if the official rate is 2%. That's because of the multiplication factor. It's compounding: 2% on this year's 2%, which really works out to be 2.04%. What this means is that if your annual yield is 4% on a three-year GIC, for example, you're guaranteed to lose after the first year.

Again, you have to look forward. Not backward. And always look at multi-dimensional ways, not just to produce yield but to provide capital gains as well to offset the inflation on your original investment.

Don't count on the government to support you. Government is being downsized at all levels. Despite this, as taxpayers we still have to pay the debts racked up by previous governments. This all adds up to one thing: Don't count on money being there for you when your turn comes. If you do, you'll be at the government's mercy. If you're in control of your own destiny, you'll be in the driver's seat.

Banks are great places — for loans. But not as a place to store your money. All you're really doing when you deposit money with a bank is providing capital for it to lend to someone else. That, after all, is the banks' business, and they're very good at it — but at your expense. So why not buy the bank — bit by bit — by acquiring its shares or, better still, by acquiring mutual funds which own bank stocks. Banks are the bedrock on which our economy and growth are based and, as such, very strong places to invest in but not to store your money in.

Prepare for bad weather. I'm talking not about El Niño but about bad economic weather. The good weather will, in fact, take care of itself. You have to prepare for the bad times. That means an umbrella if you plan to go out in the rain. A bank will give you an umbrella on a sunny day. But most of us need an umbrella for the bad times, too. My investment strategies are based on this premise. So should yours be.

Treat your investments the same way you would treat your family. With respect. You should look at your investments as if you were buying a big-ticket item like a new TV. Most of us will buy colour — the latest state-of-the-art model. Not a black-and-white set that was common in the 1960s.

The same principle applies to investing. The financial world is undergoing massive changes. So is the world of investing. If I were thinking about investing in a GIC, for example, it would be in a state-of-the-art GIC. Not one that just pays interest. That's one-dimensional, and the income is fully taxable. Today you might want to consider a convertible GIC — one that can be converted into a mutual fund — an important option if your investment ideas happen to change down the road or if it's obvious the stock market is getting ready to take off. Bottom line is that you don't want to be locked in to any one position. That's the positioning I talked about earlier.

Keeping abreast of the latest financial products is a key part of this process — if only to ensure that you do not expose yourself to any undue risk. For example, the guaranteed income fund — a type of mutual fund that will enable you to lock in and guarantee your principal plus any profits you may have at any time.

If you invested $10,000 in one of these funds, and it went up by 10% or $1,000, you could lock in $11,000. If it rose another 10% the following year, you would be able to lock in $12,100 by cancelling the original guarantee and putting in a new guarantee. There is a catch, however. You must hold the fund 10 years every time you lock in. That's state-of-the-art financial planning — new, less risky investments that will give you long-term growth at virtually no risk.

These are some of the rules that I live by and that have helped me along the way. I know they will help to create a prosperous future for you, too.